PEOPLE IN THE NEWS

Sting

by Anne E. Hill

LUCENT BOOKS®

San Diego • Detroit • New York • San Francisco • Cleveland
New Haven, Conn. • Waterville, Maine • London • Munich

To Caleb, we loved you before we even met you.

© 2003 by Lucent Books. Lucent Books is an imprint of The Gale Group, Inc., a division of Thomson Learning, Inc.

Lucent Books® and Thomson Learning™ are trademarks used herein under license.

For more information, contact
Lucent Books
27500 Drake Rd.
Farmington Hills, MI 48331-3535
Or you can visit our Internet site at http://www.gale.com

ALL RIGHTS RESERVED.
No part of this work covered by the copyright hereon may be reproduced or used in any form or by any means—graphic, electronic, or mechanical, including photocopying, recording, taping, Web distribution, or information storage retrieval systems—without the written permission of the publisher.

LIBRARY OF CONGRESS CATALOGING-IN-PUBLICATION DATA

Hill, Anne E., 1974—
  Sting / by Anne E. Hill.
   p. cm. — (People in the news)
  Includes bibliographical references (p.) and index.
  Summary: Profiles the life of Sting, including his education, his music and acting career, success, and future plans.
   ISBN 1-56006-981-3 (alk. paper)
   1. Sting (Musician)—Juvenile literature. 2. Rock musicians—Great Britain—Biography—Juvenile literature. [1. Sting (Musician) 2. Musicians. 3. Rock music.] I. Title. II. People in the news (San Diego, Calif.)
    ML3930.S77 H5 2003
    782.42166'092—dc21
                                                                           2002005161

Printed in the United States of America

Table of Contents

Foreword	4
Introduction	
An Englishman on the Charts	6
Chapter 1	
Humble Beginnings	9
Chapter 2	
Finding His Way	21
Chapter 3	
Sting and The Police	32
Chapter 4	
The Price of Fame	46
Chapter 5	
Musician Turned Actor	59
Chapter 6	
Solo Pursuits	68
Notes	82
Important Dates in the Life of Sting	85
For Further Reading	88
Works Consulted	90
Index	92
Picture Credits	96
About the Author	96

Foreword

FAME AND CELEBRITY are alluring. People are drawn to those who walk in fame's spotlight, whether they are known for great accomplishments or for notorious deeds. The lives of the famous pique public interest and attract attention, perhaps because their experiences seem in some ways so different from, yet in other ways so similar to, our own.

Newspapers, magazines, and television regularly capitalize on this fascination with celebrity by running profiles of famous people. For example, television programs such as *Entertainment Tonight* devote all of their programming to stories about entertainment and entertainers. Magazines such as *People* fill their pages with stories of the private lives of famous people. Even newspapers, newsmagazines, and television news frequently delve into the lives of well-known personalities. Despite the number of articles and programs, few provide more than a superficial glimpse of their subjects.

Lucent's People in the News series offers young readers a deeper look into the lives of today's newsmakers, the influences that have shaped them, and the impact they have had in their fields of endeavor and on other people's lives. The subjects of the series hail from many disciplines and walks of life. They include authors, musicians, athletes, political leaders, entertainers, entrepreneurs, and others who have made a mark on modern life and who, in many cases, will continue to do so for years to come.

These biographies are more than factual chronicles. Each book emphasizes the contributions, accomplishments, or deeds that have brought fame or notoriety to the individual and shows how that person has influenced modern life. Authors portray their subjects in a realistic, unsentimental light. For example, Bill Gates—the cofounder and chief executive officer of the software giant Microsoft—has been instrumental in making personal computers the most vital tool of the modern age. Few dispute his business savvy, his perseverance, or his technical expertise, yet critics say he is ruthless in his dealings with competitors and driven more by his desire to maintain Microsoft's dominance in the computer industry than by an interest in furthering technology.

In these books, young readers will encounter inspiring stories about real people who achieved success despite enormous obstacles. Oprah Winfrey—the most powerful, most watched, and wealthiest woman on television today—spent the first six years of her life in the care of her grandparents while her unwed mother sought work and a better life elsewhere. Her adolescence was colored by promiscuity, pregnancy at age fourteen, rape, and sexual abuse.

Each author documents and supports his or her work with an array of primary and secondary source quotations taken from diaries, letters, speeches, and interviews. All quotes are footnoted to show readers exactly how and where biographers derive their information, and provide guidance for further research. The quotations enliven the text by giving readers eyewitness views of the life and accomplishments of each person covered in the People in the News series.

In addition, each book in the series includes photographs, annotated bibliographies, timelines, and comprehensive indexes. For both the casual reader and the student researcher, the People in the News series offers insight into the lives of today's newsmakers—people who shape the way we live, work, and play in the modern age.

Introduction

An Englishman on the Charts

STING HAS BEEN in the news for more than two decades–since his group The Police's 1978 single "Roxanne" hit the airwaves. In the more than twenty years that have followed, he has proven to be one of the world's most popular and enduring musical performers. His music, both with The Police and as a solo artist, has been met with acclaim and awards. He has performed at the Super Bowl, been awarded a star on Hollywood's Walk of Fame,

From his early days as front man for The Police, (pictured) Sting (center) has evolved into one of the most popular and critically acclaimed solo artists.

been inducted into the National Academy of Popular Music's Songwriters Hall of Fame, and earned two Academy Award nominations for Best Song.

But few people know the real Sting, the one behind his performances and awards. That is because Sting has been guarded about what he reveals to the public. He learned about protecting his privacy after his success with The Police and has preferred to live a quiet, although privileged, life with his wife and children. However, he still takes a shine to the spotlight. In July 2000, he told *Vanity Fair* magazine that his idea of perfect happiness is "singing my head off."[1]

And that is what he does and has been doing since he was a young boy growing up in Wallsend, Newcastle upon Tyne, England. Sting knew he was determined to be more than a shipbuilder, as so many men in his shipyard town were, or a milkman, like his father. But Sting's future seemed questionable as he struggled in school and showed little promise in anything other than sports or music. His early efforts at music did not seem promising and he bounced from group to group, never seeming to find his place with any of them—until The Police.

Fortunately, Sting's love for music has more than paid off. But fame has not been without its costs. Temptation has presented itself and Sting has not always been strong. Like many musicians and celebrities, he struggled with drugs and alcohol. His infidelity to his first wife created marital problems that led to their divorce.

However, Sting has now found the life that is best for him. He eats well, exercises (and includes yoga and meditation in his routines), and does not smoke or do drugs. He is also very much in love with Trudie Styler, his second wife and mother of four of his children. The two have made family the center of their life together and divide their time among several homes all over the world.

But through it all, there has been music. In his nearly twenty-five-year career, Sting's music has been difficult to classify. He has been influenced by classical and jazz music as well as rock, country, and reggae. And each of Sting's successful songs, including "Roxanne," "Every Breath You Take," and "Fragile," all contain a little bit of his personal thoughts and feelings. Early in his career, in 1983, Sting revealed to a *Rolling Stone* reporter:

Sting gestures to the crowd at a 2001 concert in Istanbul. In the third decade of his career, Sting shows no signs of fading from the limelight.

My personal life is in my songs, in an archetypal form, of course. At the same time, I regard myself as quite a complicated person, and there are very complex things going on in my head. Many of the songs seem quite contradictory, and I seem to be two people: on the one hand, a morose, doom-laden character, and on the other, a happy-go-lucky maniac.[2]

While the majority of stories about Sting have understandably been about his music, Sting is much more than just lyrics and notes. He is an actor who has starred in movies like *Dune* and *The Bride*, an activist who tirelessly supports Amnesty International and saving the Brazilian rain forests, and the father of six children.

Now in his fifties, Sting shows no sign of slowing down or even aging. To many, Sting is more youthful, energetic, and creative than ever. "No one's been able to come up to me with a limit," Sting says on his official website. "They've tried, but I've always been able to duck and weave, and I'm still doing that."[3]

Chapter 1

Humble Beginnings

STING'S LIFE STARTED out showing no indication that he would one day become a rock star. The dreary, industrial town of Wallsend, Newcastle upon Tyne, England, where his parents lived, stressed hard work and little indulgence like vacations or new clothes. Music was one of the last things that concerned the citizens of Wallsend. They were too worried about putting food on the table and having a roof over their heads. No famous person had ever come from Wallsend. Most people lived there quietly their whole lives and performed low-paying, menial jobs.

Sting grew up in the industrial town of Wallsend, a municipality of Newcastle upon Tyne (pictured).

But one boy would become the exception and put Wallsend on the map.

Growing up, even Sting's real name did not seem fit for a rock star. He was born Gordon Matthew Sumner on October 2, 1951, the first child of Ernest and Audrey Sumner.

Life in Wallsend

Wallsend, Newcastle upon Tyne, is located three hours north of London. Like many towns in northern England, life was not easy there. The region is known for hard times, poverty, and gray skies.

But it had not always been that way. In the early 1900s, the town was known for coal and steel mining and shipbuilding. Business was booming through the first and second world wars because the town helped produce many of the ships needed.

But after World War II, by the time Gordon was born, unemployment had gripped the area. There was no longer a need for warships and, because most workers in the town had been employed by this single industry, people suddenly found themselves out of work.

The town was already behind the times in many respects. Many people still used horses to get around even though cars had been used in most parts of the world for years. The depressed economic situation did not help improve life there.

In addition, the weather was gloomy in Wallsend—full of cold, gray days and not much sunshine, which matched the mood Gordon had while he lived there. He was not alone in his restlessness, however. Many young people living in post–World War II Europe felt disillusioned. Their dissatisfaction with economic and political conditions led to the social upheavals of the 1960s. Many musicians at the time, like the Beatles, led the movement to invoke change.

But before he too could start inciting change, Gordon was just a regular English boy. Luckily, his father Ernest did have a job (unlike many of his less-fortunate neighbors) as a milkman, a person who delivered milk from door to door. Although the job did not pay well, it allowed his family to rent a flat and eat three meals a day.

Humble Beginnings 11

Audrey also contributed some money to household expenses as a hairdresser and then as a nurse. Known as a great beauty in the town, Audrey Cowell was just a teenager when she married Ernest Sumner, and she was only eighteen when Gordon was born. She prided herself on her good looks and wanted her son to make an appropriate match with a pretty girl. (She might have placed too much emphasis on looks and not enough on substance, however, as Gordon had a reputation for loving and leaving the prettiest girls.)

Gordon was very attached to his mother and his first impressions of women were based on his mother's own looks and her opinions of girls. Sting recalls that his mother attracted whistles and admiring looks from men as she walked down the streets of Wallsend on her way to the market or to work.

Of course, it was difficult for Audrey to find time to work after the Sumners had another boy, Philip, and two girls, Angela and Anita. The Sumners struggled financially, which put a strain on the already tense relationship between the parents. As a young boy, Sting remembers that his parents constantly fought over money. He worried that they would split up. (Ernie and Audrey eventually did separate, but not until their children were grown up and out of the house.)

Despite his unhappiness at the time, Sting claims he does not have terrible memories of his childhood (although ironically he often says he was unhappy for much of it).

> It gave me a fighting spirit. I didn't have an unusually bad childhood, it's just that I have a certain mentality [perspective on life] that made childhood very painful. I remember aching–there was just an ache all the time. Heartache. It wasn't my parents' fault, it's just the way my brain was working.[4]

But of course, as a young boy, all Gordon knew was life in Wallsend. And he tried as hard as he could to escape it. Any way to forget his family troubles and how bleak life was in his neighborhood was a welcome diversion to him.

He turned to the family's black-and-white television set as much as possible. He loved adventure series and playing make-believe on the streets outside his home. Once he learned to read, he had another way to escape in the pages of books like the classics *Ivanhoe*, Sir Walter Scott's story of medieval England, or *Treasure Island*, the famous Robert Louis Stevenson novel about ships and pirates. He read everything he could and even began writing stories of his own. His ability to write well would come in handy when he started writing songs years later.

The Student

Gordon's days of unhappiness at home were soon replaced by days of unhappiness at school. He hated school and every subject he was taught except English. He could write well from an early age and spelling tests brought out Gordon's competitive

Humble Beginnings 13

nature. He enjoyed "performing" in front of his classmates in the school's spelling bees. But this was not enough to make him look forward to going to school every day.

In addition to not enjoying what he was learning, Gordon was not very popular at school either. He had few friends but seemed to enjoy being a loner. He preferred to read rather than goof off with the other kids. This did not earn him any friends. One schoolmate remembered, "Literacy, in those days, wasn't necessarily an asset."[5] In other words, being academic (good at school) was not something to which most kids aspired.

Despite his love for books, Gordon spent much of his time daydreaming his way through class instead of paying attention to his teachers. He saved all of his creative energy for home where he wrote his own stories that no one else read.

Besides his love for reading, Gordon had another quality that made him stand out: He was very tall for his age and this made him the butt of many jokes. He was called Lurch after the freakishly tall character on *The Addams Family* television series.

Unusually tall for his age, the young Gordon was known to his classmates as Lurch. Lurch, pictured here as a chauffeur, is the gargantuan butler of The Addams Family *television show.*

By the time he was eleven, Gordon was fighting with his teachers and was considered a troublemaker, even though he had proven he could excel in the classroom if he chose. The local public school he attended just did not challenge him or make him happy.

But bigger and better things were waiting for him at St. Cuthbert's Grammar School, a more prestigious Catholic school in a nearby town to which he was accepted. Finally, he was out of Wallsend for much of the year. (Ironically, even though Gordon disliked the classroom, he ended up teaching for a few years.)

In addition to going to classes, students at St. Cuthbert's also attended Mass. Growing up Catholic was something that Sting never questioned as a child but reflected on later as an adult:

> I was raised Catholic. And in the rock world, which is *hedonistic* [pleasure-seeking], and on the surface very *existential* [free from moral consideration], it sets you apart to have had an upbringing that was rooted in magic and religion. I'm not a devout Catholic and I don't go to Mass, but I'm not sure I've broken away from it. All that was inculcated into my brain as a small child–that there is a heaven and hell, mortal sins and venial sins–is inside my psyche, and will never come out.[6]

Sting on Becoming a Priest

Few people can imagine Sting as anything but a musician. And with stories that he had been unfaithful to his first wife and used drugs and alcohol, the priesthood seemed an unlikely calling. However, when he was a boy, Gordon actually considered this profession. In 1996, Sting told *Interview* reporter David Furnish:

> I was brought up Roman Catholic and I served on the altar [was an altar boy]. So I have a history of religious education. For perverse reasons, I even toyed with the idea of becoming a priest at one point. I won't go into that. Then I got into existentialism and intellectual agnosticism [acknowledging that you are not sure there is a God] and then atheism [believing that there is no God]. Now I'm sort of reverting back to the idea that religion is important.

The Athlete

Another part of Sting that still exists today and started as a child is his athleticism. "I was fit to start with," the singer has said. "[S]o I have managed to stay that way."[7] Of course, as a boy and young teen, Gordon cared less about staying in shape and more about having fun. Gordon was also competitive by nature and this helped him in his drive to win sporting events in which he competed. This competitive streak helped him later on while he was pursuing a career as a musician. He was unwilling to give up and determined to succeed.

Instead of team sports, Sting liked to compete one-on-one. His brother Philip was a fan of football (which is known as soccer in the United States), but Gordon preferred the solitary sport of running. He would observe, learn from, and imitate his opponents on the track. He was soon a Northumberland running champion in both the one-hundred and two-hundred meters. At age nineteen he even ran the one-hundred-meter race in 10.4 seconds (which is not far off the world record of 9.84 seconds set by Canadian sprinter and Olympic champion Donovan Bailey in 1996).

Experimenting with Drugs and Sex

But Gordon the athlete was never totally serious about sports either. It was just another thing he was good at without trying too hard. And so, out of boredom, he took an interest in other activities like trying drugs and alcohol.

Many kids Gordon's age were experimenting with illegal substances. But because he looked older than his classmates, Gordon was often found inside pubs drinking beer instead of sneaking drinks from his parents' home. For Gordon, drinking led to drug use.

Although trying marijuana and amphetamines and drinking alcohol did not exactly help on the track or in the classroom, Gordon enjoyed the mind-altering effects. He felt he could escape his unhappy home life by drinking and using drugs.

He used drugs casually for many years—even after he became a famous musician. He later said: "I don't believe people who say, 'I can handle it. I've been taking drugs since I was twelve.'

It's wrong, and as Puritan as it might sound, they're not even that much fun."[8]

A few years after he started drinking and trying drugs, Gordon also tried something else–sex. Although Gordon still did not have many friends, he had finally grown into his looks and many girls were attracted to him. He lost his virginity and soon began lots of casual sexual relationships with girls he met. In the late 1960s (the era of "free love"), Acquired Immune Deficiency Syndrome (AIDS) was not yet known and most people knew little about sexually transmitted diseases (STDs) in general. Although Gordon wanted to find a girl to relate to and call his girlfriend, he had trouble connecting emotionally with any of the girls he met. Instead, there was empty sex and even allegations of pregnancy by some of his sexual partners.

Sex was yet another way for Gordon to remove himself from the present. All these things helped him forget that he was dissatisfied. Gordon was happy to escape his own life, even for a little while. Like many young people experiencing the challenges of adolescence, he just felt like he did not belong anywhere. He had not found his niche and he was filling his days with the wrong kinds of activities.

But that changed as soon as he became interested in music. He found his salvation from life in Wallsend and finally overcame his angst when he learned to play the guitar and write songs.

The Aspiring Musician

Audrey loved playing the piano and she introduced her young son to the instrument when he was very young. It left an impression on Gordon. He later recalled in a commencement address at the Berklee College of Music in 1994:

> My earliest memory is also my earliest musical memory. I remember sitting at my mother's feet as she played the piano. . . . The piano was an upright with worn brass pedals. And when my mother played one of her tangos she seemed to be transported to another world. Her feet rocking rhythmically between loud and soft pedals, her arms pumping to the odd rhythms of the tango, her eyes

intent upon the sheet music in front of her. For my mother, playing the piano was the only time I wasn't the center of her world–the only time she ignored me. So I knew that something significant–some important ritual was being enacted here. I suppose I was being initiated into something–ignited into some sort of mystery. The mystery of music.[9]

Gordon wanted to play the piano too, but he did not seem to have a knack for it. He practiced nearly every day, but knew his attempts left a lot to be desired. Then the family piano had to be sold to pay off a debt and neither mother nor son could play anymore.

When he was eight, Gordon's uncle left an old Spanish guitar at the Sumner house and Gordon became obsessed with learning how to play it. "He used to drive us mad [crazy] with

The Influence of the Beatles

While Gordon listened to many kinds of music as a youngster, one group influenced him more than any other: the British group the Beatles. The Beatles were the most popular group in England and the United States in the 1960s and sold millions of albums. The Police actually went on to sell even more albums than the Beatles did during their career. But Sting's admiration of the "Fab Four," as the members of the Beatles were called, is no less now than what it was then. He explained in a 1994 commencement address at the Berklee College of Music:

> There was only one radio station in England at that time [when I was young]—the BBC. And you could hear the Beatles and the Rolling Stones side by side with bits of Mozart, Beethoven, Glenn Miller and even the blues. This was my musical education. It's eclecticism, supplemented by my parents' record collection of Rodgers and Hammerstein, Lerner and Lowe, Elvis Presley, Little Richard and Jerry Lee Lewis. But it wasn't until the Beatles that I realized perhaps I could make a living out of music.
>
> The Beatles came from the same working-class background as I did. They were English, and Liverpool [a town in northwest England, where the Beatles were from] wasn't any fancier or more romantic than my own home town. And my guitar went from being the companion of my solitude to the means of my escape.

that guitar,"[10] Audrey later said. But unlike the piano, Gordon seemed to have a knack for this instrument. After Gordon strummed the guitar for several hours a week, Ernie finally consented to let him take music lessons. But Gordon struggled with these.

Although he showed tremendous talent, Gordon would not conform to the music teacher's rigid tastes of playing certain kinds of a music in a very particular way. Ernie refused to pay the money for lessons if his son was not going to cooperate with the teacher, so Gordon was back to learning on his own–which was exactly what he preferred.

Sting recalls: "I didn't feel as if I belonged anywhere. I think that fed my creativity. I sought solace in music and playing the guitar or songwriting or simply in fantasy. I'd be off in my own world which then became my career."[11]

But before his career could take off, Gordon had a lot to learn about different kinds of music and musical styles (which he would later call on to write songs). Gordon enjoyed listening to his favorite kinds of music and musicians–especially jazz. He had always been a huge fan of this musical form, which is an American style of music that stresses improvisation (making up the music while playing) and features many instruments.

Gordon especially liked Thelonious Monk and Charles Mingus. Soon, the strains of soul and rock music could also be heard coming from Gordon's bedroom whenever he was home. He loudly played popular music by the Beatles and James Taylor, but was influenced by just about everything and everyone he heard.

But nothing that came out of Gordon's stereo could compare to live music. In 1965, when he was just thirteen, he saw his first live musical performance by jazz-blues group the Graham Bond Organization at a local club called Club a Go Go. Over the years, he also saw rock groups like Manfred Mann, Cream, the Animals, and Pink Floyd perform there, as well as musician Jimi Hendrix. Little did the teen know that he would someday be as famous as the groups of musicians he idolized.

But Gordon was not content just listening to music and watching other musicians perform. He, too, wanted to be a performer. He often locked himself in the bedroom he shared with his brother and played the guitar; he even began writing his

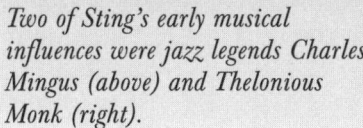
Two of Sting's early musical influences were jazz legends Charles Mingus (above) and Thelonious Monk (right).

own songs. Most of his songs were full of longing and the suffering he was feeling in Wallsend–where he never felt he belonged. Sting is not the first musician to have felt alienated or out of place as a teenager. Some musicians have written their best songs about feeling lonely and isolated, especially Sting. He says, "I continued to write about that kind of pain and loneliness until I was successful [as a musician]."[12]

Problems with His Parents

There were many roadblocks, however, on Gordon's long road to becoming successful at music. As a teen, the biggest obstacle he faced was his parents. Like most teens, he was often moody and sometimes rebellious, but he really just wanted attention.

Gordon lived to please his father but Ernie never seemed to give his older son the approval and affection he was always looking for. Sting says, "In his generation you didn't show your feelings or even hug your children. I grew up thinking that was the way to behave."[13] (Sting now makes sure he tells his children he loves them every day so they have the affection he did not receive from his father.)

When Gordon brought home a ribbon from a track meet, his father would not congratulate him or tell him he was proud. In fact, a rivalry (more common between siblings) developed between the two. Gordon's father would sometimes join his teenage son in playing the guitar after work and when he had free time. Soon, it was a musical battle between father and son as Gordon tried to show his father how much he was improving. Instead of feeling proud that his son was surpassing him, Ernie became annoyed. The jam sessions quickly ended on a sour note.

But Gordon was not ready to give up on a relationship with his father. He accompanied his father on his milk delivery route to get to know him better, but even this did not create a bond between them. Ernie thought Gordon was too sensitive and tender, that he did not act like a man. Sadly, Ernie just did not understand his artistic older son.

Luckily, Audrey did. The mother and son were very close, and she heaped on the praise that Ernie refused to give. Audrey urged Gordon to date their neighbors' pretty daughters, and she took great pride in the fact that her son was growing up to be tall and handsome.

But this close relationship between the two almost ended one day when Gordon refused to come down to the dinner table. He was playing his music–as always–and did not want to be disturbed. Audrey and Ernie had a fight over Gordon's refusal to come downstairs, and Ernie ordered his wife to make their disobedient son come to the table. When Audrey's pleas to Gordon did not work, Ernie was ready to go up and force his son downstairs. But Audrey got upstairs first. Frustrated and angry, she grabbed the guitar from Gordon's hands and smashed it into pieces.

Gordon was shocked by what his mom had done, but he did not take his anger out on her. He simply went downstairs and walked out the front door. He did not return for two days. He made up his mind that he needed to get out of Wallsend and music seemed to be his only escape.

Chapter 2

Finding His Way

ALTHOUGH GORDON SUMNER planned to be a musician, he had enough sense to realize that he might not succeed. After all, most people never left Wallsend, let alone went on to become famous musicians.

The seventeen-year-old needed a fallback plan. So he decided to attend college. School was not the path he wanted to take, but it seemed like a safe way out.

That is, until Gordon got his test results back and learned that they were good enough for only a few colleges—none of which interested him. Instead, he seemed doomed to a life of low-paying jobs in his old hometown.

Life After High School

In 1969, Gordon returned home to live with his parents. After attending school and living on his own for much of the year, this was an adjustment for the nearly eighteen-year-old. Life was as dreary as ever in Wallsend, even though his family had moved and was now living in a nicer, middle-class home. His father also owned his own small dairy so money was less of an urgent issue—at least for the elder Sumners.

Because he was no longer in school, Gordon was now faced with making a living for himself. He briefly attended Warwick University but hated it and dropped out. For more than a year he had various jobs, such as a ditchdigger and a bus conductor, but he did not hold any of them for longer than a few months. Music was the only constant in his life, but even though Gordon formed several bands with friends, his musical ability was not paying the bills.

Sting performs his 1988 concert at London's Wembley Arena. Before realizing his dream of becoming a successful musician, Sting aspired to be a teacher.

Ernest was getting more frustrated with his older son and their fights were getting worse. Ernest did not approve of Gordon's jobs, his clothes, or his hair. (Gordon became caught up in the "mod," or modern, late 1960s fashions and wore suede, bell-bottoms, and long hair.)

Finally, after floating from job to job and not finding one he enjoyed enough to keep, Gordon applied to Northern Counties Teacher Training College and was accepted for the fall 1971 term. He decided to pursue his teacher's certificate in English and music (his two favorite subjects). Even though Gordon did not like formal schooling, he liked the idea of helping other kids and making their time in school easier than his own had been.

When he was not working, Gordon liked to hang out at the local pub in his parents' neighborhood and even played bass guitar with the house band when it needed a substitute. Gordon loved performing, but thought he would never find someone else his own age who enjoyed it as much as he did. He was wrong.

Meeting Gerry Richardson

Gordon soon met the person who would most influence his fledgling musical career, a young man named Gerry Richardson.

Gerry, a fellow aspiring musician who was a year ahead of Gordon at the teachers college, was also studying English. Gerry sang and loved jazz music. He also played keyboards with a local jazz band. When the lead singer of the band told Gerry that she had seen a great new talent singing and playing James Taylor ballads on his bass guitar at a local pub, Gerry went to watch and listen to Gordon play. "I went along and thought he was all right," he later explained. "I didn't give a toss [care] about Sting's bass playing until we got talking and I discovered he knew a drummer who owned a van and a PA [public address system]. That's what I really wanted so I sacked my bassist and drummer and we formed this new line-up called Earthrise."[14]

Gerry's and Gordon's personalities clicked and the two became fast friends. They even got an apartment together near the school. Finally, Gordon had met someone who loved music as much as he did—someone who was serious about a career in music. While Earthrise was hardly a well-known band, it did perform for audiences and even got paid sometimes. At long last, Gordon could finally say he was a working musician and a permanent member of an actual group.

Gordon Gets His Nickname

Gordon had only been performing with Earthrise for a short while when he left to join another, bigger group called Phoenix. This group was better known and played Gordon's first love in music: traditional jazz. He was introduced to the members of Phoenix by Gerry, who sometimes filled in when they needed a keyboardist.

It was the members of Phoenix who gave Gordon his now famous nickname that he has gone by ever since—and it was all by chance. For his first rehearsal with the band, Gordon wore

Sting acquired his nickname when a band mate observed that his favorite yellow-and-black striped shirt made him look like a bumblebee.

his favorite yellow-and-black striped shirt. Someone suggested that he looked like a bee. Because none of the members of the group went by their own names and preferred nicknames instead, Gordon became "Sting." Gordon had never really liked his own name, so Sting was fine with him.

Sting fit in with Phoenix and finally seemed content, but other musicians in different groups noticed his talents as well. Other groups tried to woo him away to play bass guitar and sing with them. Even though he enjoyed playing with Phoenix, the Newcastle Big Band succeeded in convincing Sting to play with them. Gerry joined the band as well. The two friends and musicians were now practically inseparable.

Now in his early twenties, Sting had played in three bands but still had not found the one with which he wanted to settle down. He did not think anyone was as serious about music as he was—or had as much talent as he thought he had. From an early age, Sting was self-confident of his abilities. He was dissatisfied with the twenty-piece Newcastle Big Band and let his opinions be known.

Finding His Way

Sting became known as a perfectionist who was concerned not only with his instrument (bass guitar) but with everyone else's as well. He was more dedicated than many of the other musicians who just seemed eager to get free drinks and meet women. Even though he got to record an album with the Newcastle Big Band that sold all of the two thousand copies made, Sting felt limited musically. The band performed what was popular at the time, so Sting found himself playing many Beatles tunes but no original songs. Sting could hear most songs once and then play them. He could cover nearly every popular song of his day, but he wanted to write his own music, rather than perform versions of existing songs.

Despite playing other people's music, Sting developed a talent for improvising and he never played a song the same way twice. On top of it all, he developed a great stage presence. Sting liked to ham it up for the crowd by gyrating and thrusting his pelvis. He never stood still while playing like some of the other musicians with whom he worked. Sometimes, however, Sting was forced to just sit or stand and play. This was frustrating for him.

The Beatles provided much of the material for the Newcastle Big Band, the twenty-piece cover band with which Sting performed early in his career.

In addition to playing with his band, Sting took other musical jobs as well. He did everything from playing music for strip dancers' routines in clubs to playing in the orchestra of a local production of Andrew Lloyd Webber's *Joseph and the Amazing Technicolor Dreamcoat*.

Forming Last Exit

Unsatisfied with playing in the Newcastle Big Band, Sting and Gerry formed their own band called Last Exit. They also recruited two older musicians to join them: guitarist John Hedley and drummer Ronnie Pearson. They believed that Hedley and Pearson were more serious than others they had worked with.

Sting played bass but also shared lead vocals with Pearson. His unusual voice and the band's unique chemistry soon had them landing regular gigs. Because the group performed original songs, Sting was finally able to introduce some songs he had written.

The group found local success and started playing regular dates at pubs around Newcastle. They were even invited to Spain for the San Sebastian Music Festival in July 1975. They then played a six-week tour up and down the Spanish coast—for very little money. The experience was valuable, however, and foreshadowed Sting's future of touring.

In addition to playing the bass guitar and sharing lead vocals, Sting had become Last Exit's main songwriter. (In fact, when Sting joined The Police and then later went solo, many of the group's members claimed his songs sounded strangely close to songs they had performed or ideas they had had as a group. But while members noticed the similarities and may have even been bitter, legal action was never taken against Sting. After all, he had been the group's songwriter.)

Back home in England, the group recorded a single of Sting singing "Whispering Voices," a song written by Gerry. Record executives and producers who attended some of the band's gigs had trouble classifying its unique blend of different kinds of music. Although they never got a record contract, the band was undeterred. They were making some money and doing what they loved. This extra money helped supplement the small sum Sting was about to start earning as a teacher after graduation.

The Graduate and Teacher

Despite having never loved, or even believed in, formal education, Sting became a full-time teacher in the fall of 1974. He was the only member of Last Exit who had a day job, but Sting actually saw teaching and performing as related. He stood in front of an audience (his class) every day to entertain and teach.

And Sting's students, all between the ages of five and nine, loved their young teacher. He urged them to call him Sting rather than Mr. Sumner. He was a different kind of teacher, especially for the religious and usually strict atmosphere at St. Paul's First School.

Sister Agnes Miller recalls: "He had a tremendous gift for talking to young children. He didn't talk to them, but more with them. . . . At break, he could often be found strumming his guitar in the assembly hall or playing the piano. The children loved him."[15] Some of these same children Sting taught later attended some of his early gigs. They were clearly smitten with their cool and handsome young teacher.

So too were some of the female staff. Despite their flirtations, Sting did not have a girlfriend and seemed to be the quintessential bachelor. He was now making money, playing music, and living on his own. Women frequented the apartment shared by Gerry and Sting and became the band's first groupies.

Even though Sting seemed to be a natural at teaching, he never really threw himself wholeheartedly into his chosen profession. He was the last teacher to arrive in the morning and the first to leave at the end of the day, usually because he had to get to a gig with Last Exit. Perhaps Sting never committed himself to teaching because he knew his future was as a musician.

Sting Falls in Love

In December 1974, one of the gigs Sting was running off to one evening was a Christmas show. Last Exit was playing *Rock Nativity*, a musical version of the Christmas story, at the University Theater.

A young Irish actress named Frances Tomelty was playing the part of the Virgin Mary. When Sting set eyes on Frances, he knew he had to get to know her. He had a feeling she could be the girlfriend he had always wanted. At the party after the show, he approached the pretty brunette and struck up a conversation. She did not seem interested in Sting at first. In fact, she had her eye on Last Exit's lead guitarist.

But Sting was persistent and his charm grew on Frances during the run of the show. They learned they both felt passionately about their careers—Frances was as devoted to her acting as

Sting kisses his first wife, actress Frances Tomelty, in this 1980 photo. The two married in 1976 and divorced in 1983.

Sting was to his music—and about politics. Frances was from Northern Ireland and had definite opinions about the Irish Republican Army (IRA) and her war-torn country. The IRA was organized almost a hundred years before Frances and Sting met, as a violent resistance to British occupation of Ireland. But the 1970s brought IRA violence in England to a new level with a series of deadly bombings at pubs, restaurants, and other public places. The romance between an Englishman and Irishwoman was not typical, as the countries were at definite odds.

When the holiday show's run was over, Frances had other acting commitments in Scotland and London. But Sting could not bear to see her go, so he started commuting back and forth from Newcastle to wherever Frances performed. Even though his schedule had been full before, twenty-three-year-old Sting was willing to do whatever he needed to do to keep twenty-seven-year-old Frances in his life.

Frances opened Sting's eyes to a new world beyond Newcastle and to a new type of woman. Before dating Frances, most women Sting had dated had been pretty, but not very bright. Frances, however, was both beautiful and intelligent. She was also feisty and did not fear disagreeing with Sting (unlike the amenable women he had been with before, who offered him no challenge). The sophisticated Frances liked films, all kinds of theater, and was interested in the growing, alternative punk movement. It did not take long for Sting to fall in love.

Even though Sting had never been the faithful type, he was committed to Frances. And she had great hopes as to the man Sting was going to be. Sting claims he would often say, "'I'm just a two-bit teacher from Newcastle.' Frances replied, 'That's not how I see you,' to which Sting hit back, 'That's not how I see me either.'"[16]

The two soon realized that they were meant to be together. On May 1, 1976, they were married in the Catholic Church, even though by now Sting did not consider himself religious. They had another reason for getting married: Frances was pregnant with the couple's first child. Their son Joseph was born on November 22, 1976.

The Political Side of Sting

Sting has felt strongly about politics since he was a teen. He later incorporated these feelings into songs. He told Kristine McKenna of *Rolling Stone* in 1983:

> I'm against politics with a capital P, but I think we have to come to terms with the reality of nuclear power. It's no good to say let's get rid of it, because we'll always have that knowledge. I really dislike this Luddite [opposed to technology] mentality of "Let's go back to nature and get rid of nuclear power," because we never will. We have to make those things safe . . . and the only way to do that is to clean out the gangsters and criminals who are running our world. And they are criminals. They're greedy, frightened, and they are endangering us. . . . We will be blown up, you know. The age of the domestic H-bombs is years away. Humans make the mistake of believing that it's their right to survive. Species die out on this planet all the time without anybody noticing. The planet will still be here, and we must lose this attitude of divine right, that something will save us, which we've developed over the centuries. The Martians aren't going to come down and save us. God isn't going to save us. We are in great danger, and it's easy to get diverted from that awareness by everyday life. And every time we spend a million dollars on defense, that danger increase[s]. Those weapons are intended for use. And what [on] earth is military superiority about? Superior to what? As a species, we're too bound up in what we consume, ignoring what consumes us. It's a madness that we have to sort out.

Performing on the High Seas

Shortly after getting married, Sting took a job with Last Exit playing on board the cruise ship *Orianna* for two weeks as the house band. The members of the band saw it as a much-needed holiday. After a lot of nagging by Gerry and Sting (who wanted the gig more than their manager did), Pearson got the band booked on board the ship.

But the band members of Last Exit were not exactly ready to trade in their love of playing rock for what the people on board really wanted to hear, like fox-trots and waltzes. The guys were even reprimanded and told to tone down their music. Fortunately, a younger crowd of people found the band and enjoyed its style, so Last Exit kept the job for the rest of the two-week cruise. They had a great time making money and getting off the ship at each port of call (the place the ship stopped) to explore each town's local pubs. (In fact, Pearson liked playing on board so much that he still plays on cruise ships today.)

It was no longer vacation time for Sting after returning home, however. The twenty-five-year-old was now a husband and father. But the real question on his mind was whether or not he would ever be a successful full-time musician.

Chapter 3

Sting and The Police

STING WAS DETERMINED to be a success, but he was finding that the demands of supporting a family were daunting. Frances had decided even before she and Sting got married that she could not live in Newcastle upon Tyne. She wanted to be in a big city like London where there were more theaters and more career opportunities in addition to cultural venues (museums, restaurants, and so on).

Sting arrives at London's Heathrow Airport after a successful U.S. tour with The Police.

Sting was secretly relieved at the thought of moving. He had wanted to spread his wings for years (since he could first remember) but only needed a push to pack his bags. Change was in the air. So much had happened to Sting in 1976, which he called "the crucial year. I decided to have this kid, live with this girl, quit my job, move to London. It was all a big trauma."[17]

With no money in the bank and a new baby to support, times were tough for the Sumners, and Last Exit was having internal problems with member infighting. Still, he persevered. It was as if he knew bigger and better things awaited him.

Recording Ambitions

Sting quit his job as a teacher and suddenly no longer had a steady paycheck. He knew that he needed to make more money at music or his family would be homeless. He felt guilty and conflicted about what to do. He wanted to be a good provider but that would mean giving up his dream and taking a desk job he knew he would hate. Music was his passion but it was not paying the bills.

Still, Sting wanted to see if he could be successful on the London music scene, even though punk and reggae were just starting to emerge—not exactly the kind of music his band played. The group had laid down tracks for a demo recording of its music in a studio in Newcastle the year before and hoped the recording would get them more work. (A demo recording is like a regular record or LP but has fewer tracks and is a cheaper way for musicians to get their music made.)

Eventually, an executive from Virgin Music's subsidiary, Virgin Records, discovered the group after watching them perform live in Newcastle. Carol Wilson convinced others at the large music company to bring the members of Last Exit down to London to record demos. After the group had finished recording an impressive eleven songs in only one day, Wilson and other Virgin executives told the members of Last Exit they would need to move to London for their careers to take off.

Sting needed little convincing. He knew he wanted to be in London and that Frances would be thrilled with the move. But the other band members were reluctant to move. Last Exit was divided.

London and the Punk Music Scene

Punk music was dominating London at the time The Police arrived on the scene. Punk music started in 1976 in London as a form of rebellion against 1970s rock and disco that young people could not relate to because it was too commercial. Young people thought this music was boring and stagnant. Punk was new, different, and exciting.

Punk music was not just music, however; it was a lifestyle. Punk music followers wore ripped clothes and dyed their hair. They believed in individuality and radical ideas about politics and lifestyle that were against the norm. Between 1976 and 1981, punk youth influenced everything from the the culture of nightclubs to the attitude on the streets of London.

The Sex Pistols, The Clash, and The Damned were some of the first bands to take the punk sound to the charts. The Sex Pistols' popularity was heightened in 1977 when they brought in bassist Sid Vicious. He became a punk music icon full of attitude and image. He had a heroin habit as well, which eventually killed him just two years later. His death signaled the beginning of the end of the punk music fad.

During the time of punk, reggae was also becoming a popular music form and a fusion of the two became evident. The Clash was one of the few punk bands to escape the decline of punk music in the early 1980s by blending reggae and pop with their punk sound.

Sting struggled between going punk and finding his own sound. At first, The Police were not taken seriously in the punk clubs, because they were too much like the "establishment"—too pop and too clean-cut. They were often booed during performances. Sting often felt forced to act like a punk rocker, even though he clearly was not one. But the group soon found their own unique crowd who enjoyed their sound of jazz, reggae, and a bit of punk.

The Sex Pistols were at the forefront of the London punk scene.

Virgin did not want to lose the songwriting talent of Sting if the group decided to turn them down. They offered him a publishing contract on all his songs and everything he would write in the future. Sting eagerly signed the contract, thrilled at the thought that he could now call himself a songwriter. He never hired a lawyer to review the papers and tell him whether the deal was a fair one—and this would eventually come back to haunt him.

He was equally excited when the other members of Last Exit finally agreed to move to London, but they changed their minds at the last minute. His boxes and bags nearly packed, Sting was more than upset with them. He knew the group would not last, but musical opportunity came knocking on his door again.

A Phone Call with Stewart Copeland

Even though Last Exit did not officially break up until the beginning of 1977, Sting had already been pursuing something new months earlier—even before he moved to London. It all started with a phone call from an American drummer named Stewart Copeland.

Copeland was a member of Curved Air, a group far more popular and well known than Last Exit. Copeland had caught a Last Exit gig when he was in Newcastle. Even though the band's performance that night had left a lot to be desired, Copeland was impressed by Sting, who really worked the crowd with his charisma, and they seemed to love him in return. He felt that Sting had a stage presence that could not be denied. Copeland called Sting that night to tell him that he was forming a new band and wanted to know if Sting was interested.

Sting, impressed with Copeland's musical experience and frustrated with the stalled career of Last Exit, agreed to join the as-yet-unnamed and unformed group that would be based in London.

Suddenly, Sting's move to the southern city made sense again. He and Frances continued packing and later in the month drove down to London. They had nowhere to live and no source of income, but Sting was hopeful that he would find success with the new group.

Struggling in London

Arriving in London, the young family temporarily went to live at the apartment of a friend of Frances. The three slept on the floor and were forced to go on welfare, or "on the dole" as it was called in London. A worried Sting kept a journal of his thoughts and fears. As months went by, he grew more and more desperate to provide for his young family. He both resented their dependence on him and wanted to help them climb their way out of the poverty they had fallen into in this new city. He wondered if he had done the right thing in moving out of Wallsend.

Sting did get a few jobs modeling clothes, thanks to an agent. The money he earned by modeling, coupled with his paltry earnings from the Virgin Records songwriting deal and what he made on the dole, allowed the family to move into a tiny basement apartment. Influenced by the largely Caribbean and Jamaican community in his new neighborhood, Sting wrote some of his early songs for The Police there.

Meanwhile, Frances became the breadwinner of the family and took nearly every acting job she was offered.

Stewart Copeland pounds out the beat on his drums. Copeland encouraged Sting to leave Newcastle to form a new band in London, which the drummer named The Police.

Sting's First Days with The Police

After being in London just a few days, Sting was eager to start playing with Copeland's new band. Actually, it was a trio, consisting of drummer Copeland, guitarist Henri Padovani, and bassist Sting.

As he had been with the members of his earlier groups, Sting was often critical of new musicians he met. He was skeptical of how serious they were and often judged their musical abilities harshly. Sting felt a bond with Copeland but had less respect for Padovani, whom Sting did not see as having much talent. Still, he was happy to be playing again.

Copeland came up with the group's new name: The Police. His father had been a trumpeter with the Glenn Miller orchestra and an army intelligence officer and later on a police officer; the name was chosen out of respect to his father and his career. Some people were confused by the name in the group's early years, thinking that its members were actually police officers. When the band became famous, donations to local police departments rose because many people still mistakenly believed The Police were affiliated with law enforcement.

In the beginning, the newly formed threesome was just eager to play in public. Several weeks after they had first rehearsed together, they had their first gig opening for an American punk singer named Cherry Vanilla at a club in Wales.

Sting was less than pleased with the performance and with the early sounds of The Police, which did not fit cleanly into any one category of music like punk, pop, or reggae. Instead, they blended all of them together, which turned out to be what made them famous later on. But at first, this held the band back.

Sting thought about quitting The Police, especially after his old friend Gerry Richardson tried to convince him to join his new band for a much higher weekly salary than he was making with The Police. But for reasons still unknown, Sting stayed with The Police. The group seemed set until one night when both Sting and Copeland agreed to lend their talents out to a new group that was playing a gig at a reunion show for the popular group, the Gong.

There, they met a talented guitarist named Andy Summers who was known for having played with Eric Burdon and the Animals and with Neil Sedaka. Summers had grown tired of playing with his band. He saw raw but untapped talent in Copeland and Sting, and a short time later convinced them that they needed to replace Padovani with him as the newest member of The Police.

Although Summers joined the group, Sting and Copeland did not have the heart to fire Padovani. He might not have been the greatest guitarist, but he was enthusiastic and easy to work with. So, the group made several appearances in 1977 as a quartet, until the arguments between the two guitarists got so heated that Padovani quit.

The first time Summers, Copeland, and Sting played together in August 1977, they knew they had found the right combination for success. The members of the group had their personal differences, but professionally they worked extremely well together. It would stay this way for many years.

"It's not an easy relationship by any means," Sting said of the group in 1983. "We're three highly autonomous [independent] individuals, and a band is an artificial alliance most of the time.

A Brief History of Reggae

Reggae music is a style that originated in Jamaica and is based on American soul music but with some twists and other influences, including New Orleans rhythm and blues, Jamaican folk music, and African rhythm. According to the website Reggaefusion.com, "The synthetic style is strictly Jamaican and includes offbeat syncopations, up-stroke guitar strums, chanted vocal patterns and lyrics associated with the religious tradition of rastafari" (the belief that the only true God is the late Ethiopian emperor Ras Tafari [Haile Selassie]). Politics and poverty are also popular subjects for reggae music.

Sting became fascinated with this style of music while living in a largely Jamaican and Caribbean neighborhood in London. Listening to this music inspired him, as it did many artists of the day.

Bob Marley and the Wailers were the most well-known reggae group in the United States and England. The popularity of Marley and the Wailers made reggae both mainstream and influential to white musicians, including The Police, Paul Simon, Eric Clapton, and UB40.

Andy Summers performs in a 1979 concert. Summers became a permanent addition to The Police when the band's original guitarist quit.

There are obviously tensions, but I think there's a great love between us and a genuine respect. I can't think of two musicians I'd rather play with. But none of us is easy to work with. It's not all buddy-buddy and never was."[18]

The Police's Commercial

The three band members were determined to make it as a group in whatever way they could. In 1977, Sting was looking for ways to supplement what he was earning, so he auditioned for a Wrigley's chewing gum commercial. He got the job only after he showed the casting directors that he could act defiantly, like a punk musician. To convince them, he jumped on a table and started spitting all over the room.

But the people in charge of the commercial also wanted a group to appear in the spot. Sting suggested The Police. There was one catch, however: The guys all had to dye their hair blond for the commercial. Sting was already blond, and redheaded Copeland agreed to it, but Summers was not too sure about the change. He was outvoted, however, and the guys went blond.

Actually, the change gave the group a needed boost commercially (by making them highly recognizable), but it did not earn them much respect from fellow musicians. They were not seen as serious rock 'n' rollers because they had sold out to do a chewing gum ad. The Police were about to convince many people that they were indeed serious.

The Police's First Album

Until the latter half of 1977, Copeland was the clear-cut leader of The Police. The group had been his idea and he wrote the majority of the songs they performed. But that soon changed.

Sting had undeniable songwriting talent. He had been coming up with catchy tunes and riffs since he was a boy. But until then, he had not written an impressive and original song that had the potential to be a hit single.

That September, the group got a gig playing in Paris but could only afford to stay in the city's red-light district, the area of town where prostitutes worked on street corners. Sting recalls: "It was the first time I'd seen prostitution on the street and those [women] were actually beautiful. I had a tune going around in my head and I imagined being in love with one of those girls. I mean, they do have fellas. How would I feel?"[19]

Inspired by what he saw, Sting wrote what was to become the group's first hit: "Roxanne." Its lyrics were considered racy for the time since it was about the taboo subject of sex for sale. It talked about a young woman selling her body on the street, told from the perspective of the young man who is in love with her and wants her to stop.

Sting is still so identified with that song that when he appeared on the sketch comedy show *Saturday Night Live* years later, the actors (along with Sting) performed a skit in which he was in an elevator and every person that came on recognized him and sang parts of "Roxanne" to the musician.

The Police record their first album, Outlandos d'Amour, *in this 1978 photograph. The album's single "Roxanne" is still one of the band's biggest hits.*

The single was part of the group's first album, *Outlandos d'Amour*, which it recorded in January 1978. Stewart's brother Miles, a successful manager, agreed to front the group the money to make the album and to manage the band after hearing "Roxanne."

Miles Copeland

Before managing The Police, Miles Copeland set up a company that managed punk acts, a musical style that was popular in the late 1970s, especially in London. Miles had helped guide his younger brother Stewart's career but was determined not to get directly involved with The Police.

After all, its music was not exactly his style and working with family could be difficult. Miles especially disliked Sting and his tendency to try to act punk (spit, snarl, and so on) in a clearly pop/rock group with only a hint of punk sound.

Over time, however, Miles was convinced that The Police could use his help. And indeed, after he started managing the group, they began to take off. He was a tough businessman but gradually earned the respect of the group—and of Sting especially. (Sting served as Miles's best man when he got married in 1981. Even after the breakup of The Police, Sting and Miles remained good friends.)

Miles took the "Roxanne" single to A&M Records and negotiated an unusual deal for the band in which it would get no advance but would receive royalties from each copy sold. It was a brilliant tactic, since the band eventually earned millions from that single alone. But it took some time for the song to catch on.

Radio stations were reluctant to play the song because of its theme. That is, until Miles booked the group a U.S. tour in late 1978 and the group's popularity took off.

The First Trip to the States

The band members were struggling to make a name for themselves in their homeland, but Miles had another idea. He thought they would be more successful in the United States, and after they returned home, they might have more fame in England as well. Sting had never been to the United States before and the group was apprehensive about the tour.

Miles had not lined up any gigs prior to their arrival. Instead, he decided they would play at as many clubs and small venues on the East Coast as possible. They had their doubts, especially after a grueling four-week tour. They lugged around their own equipment, set it up, and lived as cheaply as possible just to break even. But there was no denying that the result was successful.

Not only did the intimate gigs introduce U.S. music fans to The Police, they got "Roxanne" airplay and the song started rising on the U.S. charts in late 1978. It even helped that some radio stations would not play the song—because of the controversy; people wanted to know what they were missing and sales of the single were boosted.

Sting did not like the United States at first. In fact, he compared it to hell. But this may be because the band was being overworked for very little pay. However, his opinion of the United States changed for the better each time he returned. Now, he genuinely loves the United States. He claims: "Unlike most Americans, I think I've probably been to most of America. When The Police started, we were touring America and staying in motels, dives, bordellos, and everything else, so I have a fairly good knowledge of the place as a traveler."[20] (The group returned to the United States the following year, after "Roxanne" was a certified hit, and played to bigger crowds at bigger venues.)

Success Back Home and on the Road

Once they returned home late in 1978 after their first U.S. tour, the band was disappointed that they had not found quite the same success in England. They were not any more well known despite the fact that people in the United States now knew who they were.

The Police pose for an A&M Records publicity shot. The trio's good looks and unique sound captivated American audiences on its first U.S. tour.

But that would soon change after they recorded their second album, *Regatta de Blanc*. Another single, also written by Sting, called "Message in a Bottle" was released, and the group started making some appearances on British television. They were finally catching on in their own country.

The band spent all of 1979 and some of 1980 touring. They were headlining rather than opening for more well-known bands. It was satisfying for the band members to know that their sound was catching on. Reporters followed and hounded them for interviews and photos. It was the biggest sign that they had arrived.

Twenty-eight-year-old Sting received the bulk of the media attention and was now considered something of a sex symbol. As the lead singer, he was the one always at the forefront of the band. Summers and Copeland did not mind all the attention lavished on Sting—at first. They were happy enough to be playing music and never complained about their lead singer. Sting did not mind the attention either. In fact, he relished it. He loved the spotlight and played it up for the camera, seductively running his fingers through his hair and fixing the camera with his serious gaze.

I Want My MTV

Music Television (MTV) revolutionized the music industry—some think for the better and others for the worse. The MTV story began in New York City in 1981. The first video played on the cable television channel was The Buggles' "Video Killed the Radio Star." For many pop stars, this may have been true, but for The Police, MTV helped boost their record sales. The group was good looking and Sting shined as the front man. Hearing their songs on the radio sparked listeners' interest, but seeing the group on television brought more record sales. The channel shaped popular taste and culture (in addition to making or breaking a song with a good video). Millions of young people looked to the channel to find out what was new and which bands and singers were the next hot thing.

In the early years of MTV, The Police's videos were in heavy rotation on the music channel. When he went solo, Sting continued to make videos to accompany his singles. Today, MTV has a lot of nonmusic programming in addition to music videos.

In addition to the reporters and would-be musicians who came to see the band play, there were the teenybopper fans who suddenly loved the group and followed them everywhere. This was largely because of Sting. The group was getting a boost in record sales due to the creation of MTV (Music Television). Suddenly, fans got to see their favorite music stars as well as hear them. And with Sting, they liked that they saw.

He had his pick of willing admirers backstage at each show and Sting took advantage of his rock-star status at each venue. Frances was back at home and Sting liked being "single" on the road.

Of course, even the most dedicated fans had trouble going everywhere the band went. They toured for sixteen months straight and played all over England, the United States, and Europe. Each time they played, the crowds were a little bigger and the venues a little larger.

The group decided to ride the wave of success and re-release some of its earlier songs, including "Can't Stand Losing You." Because their earlier releases had garnered little attention, everyone thought they were new singles and they sold as quickly as "Roxanne" had. The Police sold two million albums and five million singles in 1979. Sting and The Police had officially arrived.

Chapter 4

The Price of Fame

STING SEEMINGLY HAD everything that he had always wanted. He had fame and a growing fortune and he was not yet thirty. But not all was well. By putting so much time and effort into his professional life, Sting no longer had much of a personal one.

He never got to see Frances and Joseph, who was by now a rambunctious toddler. The band members, who had always thrived on creative tension, were fighting, and they blamed Sting for many of the disagreements. He had quickly developed a

Sting displays his keys as he proudly points to the make of his first car. The success of The Police brought the performer tremendous riches and fame.

rock-star ego even bigger than his band mates'. The fact that he was seen as the front man only fed his belief that The Police were not much without him.

In addition, with his every move being chronicled in the tabloids, Sting became moody and lashed out at reporters and even people he loved. He realizes this now, but he did not at the time. "When you're a rock star, you're allowed to be a petulant child and many other things you're supposed to grow out of,"[21] Sting said in 1983.

Problems of a Rock Star

The Police continued to tour the world in 1980 and also released a third album entitled *Zenyatta Mondatta* that produced two more hit singles: "Don't Stand So Close to Me" and "De Do Do Do, De Da Da Da." This was the group's first album to go platinum (meaning it sold more than one million copies) in the United States. It was now an international group.

Critics admired the group's latest efforts as well. *Rolling Stone* said *Zenyatta Mondatta* was the group's most diverse offering to date:

> [It] offers near-perfect pop by a band that bends all the rules and sometimes makes musical mountains out of molehill-size ideas. Like "Reggatta de Blanc's" "Walking on the Moon" and "The Bed's Too Big Without You" the new LP's "When the World Is Running Down, You Make the Best of What's Still Around" is based on a hypnotic three-chord progression that's repeated for almost four minutes. But the subtly dramatic rises and falls of Sting's vocal, the ricochet effect of Summers' reverberating guitar and Copeland's clipped dance beat create a melodic mirage of music and mood that lasts a long time. Much longer than the momentary upbeat charm of, say, "De Do Do Do, De Da Da Da." The latter tune is blessed with a strong hook and a quirky guitar figure too good to waste on baby talk.[22]

He should have been riding high, but Sting was already dissatisfied with fame. He started taking drugs to escape the emptiness he was feeling. (Even though he was now successful, he still felt the same way he had as a boy in Wallsend.) Miles Copeland disapproved of taking drugs, but the band members were confronted with opportunities at every turn. Most parties after the shows had lots of drugs and alcohol and the guys were offered illegal substances almost daily.

Some of the drugs, like the depressant marijuana, also kept Sting from feeling paranoid about his safety. The crowds grew at every show and fans did not leave him alone. Sting was forced to hire a bodyguard to provide protection from the screaming fans determined to touch him. It was all proving too much for Sting. He had conflicted feelings of guilt over the excessive

The Police wrestle playfully by the Thames River in this 1979 photograph. Fame and fortune led the band into a lifestyle centered around sex, drugs, and alcohol.

lifestyle he was leading, full of money, drugs, and women, and of anger at being constantly in the public eye and feeling he did not have much control over his life. He had been raised in a modest, working-class neighborhood and here he was with the ability to buy whatever he wanted. It was strange and surreal. He also felt bad about all the women he slept with to fill his lonely nights away from his family, but he did not stop.

Life on the road stretched on, with no end in sight. The group members fought more with each passing day over everything from where the group was headed in terms of a long-term career to normal everyday sibling-rivalry type arguments that brothers who spend too much time together might have.

Part of the group's life on the road was chronicled in a video-documentary called *Police Around the World.* No doubt, having cameras around all the time made Sting still more on edge. But even the most intrusive cameras could not get the full picture. The media showed him as the group's charismatic leader. But in reality, Sting was depressed, moody, and self-destructive. He needed an escape and he found it.

Sting's Fitness Obsession

In the midst of all the craziness, Sting started something new: getting in shape. He has always been athletic, but late nights performing and days touring had let him grow soft. Ironically, Sting started getting fit when he was heavily using drugs and alcohol, in The Police's early days.

Sting is now known as one of the most fit rock stars despite the fact that he is twice the age of many singers on the charts today.

Sting's daily routine includes running and practicing yoga and meditation for as many as three hours a day. Sting admitted that he had not thought much of yoga at first and could only think of old ladies sitting around hardly breaking a sweat. But Sting actually found out that yoga was a hard workout and soon it was his favorite form of exercise. He claims that staying fit also keeps him sane. He needed all the help he could get to keep it together as the band's popularity grew.

What Sting Learned About Fame

Sting learned a lot about fame after The Police became musical sensations. As the group's front man, he received most of the attention. He told *Rolling Stone* reporter Kristine McKenna in 1983 that the most important thing he had learned about being so popular was:

[t]o be more cagey. Candidly, that article you wrote quoted some things I said about my childhood that hurt my family deeply. ["I come from a family of losers . . . and I've rejected my family as something I don't want to be like."] I learned a big lesson there and had to work very hard to repair the damage done by the article. It wasn't your fault; it was purely my arrogance and lack of thought. I've become more aware of the possible consequences of what I say to the press. My family was completely unprepared for the media onslaught they were subjected to. I'm protected from it, but the innocent bystanders—my kids, my wife—were crunched by it. There's no way I can protect those around me from my career, and I have to live my own life. But there is a balance you can strike between being selfish in the right way and protecting those around you.

Troubled Singer-Songwriter

Despite his internal struggles and unhappiness, Sting continued to perform and write at a frantic pace. The early 1980s were The Police's glory days and when Sting wrote some of his best songs. What few people knew was that some of these songs were accidental—one was even fueled by a drinking binge. Sting got the idea for the hit single "Walking on the Moon" after walking around his hotel room drunk and trying not to fall down. Days later, he remembered what he had sung but wisely decided to title the song "Walking on the Moon" rather than "Walking 'Round the Room."

Sting also decided on the title for the group's fourth album *Ghost in the Machine*, released in 1981, which was also the title of a book by Arthur Koestler that Sting had been reading. The book addressed Koestler's view that the emotional part of the brain and the part that controls reason do not always work together, which is why there is violence, paranoia, and insanity in the world.

The album focused on Sting's newfound environmental and worldwide concerns with "One World" and "Spirits in the Material World," but the hit single that came from the October release was the love song "Every Little Thing She Does Is Magic."

Despite the steady success of the group, the fighting continued between members, particularly between Stewart Copeland and Sting. Miles did his best to mediate the arguments between his brother and the band's star. But after months of constant touring, it was decided that the group needed a break. It was Sting's first vacation in years. He returned home to his wife and son.

Marriage Difficulties

By mid-1980, Sting owned two luxury homes. The dank and dark basement apartment he had started out in was now just a memory. After all, he was now earning millions of dollars a year. Frances and Joe could divide their time between a large house in north London and one in west Ireland. (The house in Ireland served two purposes: moving Frances back to her homeland and saving Sting thousands of dollars in taxes by allowing him to be a resident of two countries.)

But Sting was hardly ever home to enjoy the fruits of his labor. He was away touring for months on end, leaving Frances and Joe on their own. Although Frances wanted Sting home more, she was a performer herself and knew that this was her husband's dream. She decided to continue to act while her husband was away. Although they no longer had financial worries, the long stretches away from each other were not easy on the family and particularly on Frances and Sting as a couple.

The rock star life does not promote being faithful to a spouse, and Sting had lots of late nights out with alcohol, drugs, and women at his disposal. Frances wanted to believe the best and convinced herself that Sting was being faithful. After all, they were Catholic and did not believe in extramarital relations.

Sting, however, was living a double life. On those rare occasions when he was home, he was a family man, and when he was on the road, he was the quintessential rock star. Frances found out about her husband's indiscretions when he talked about his sex life with a reporter and revealed that he needed to have sex

The band poses at a Hammersmith venue in west London. The temptations of life on the road frequently caused Sting to be unfaithful to his wife, Frances.

every night before he went to sleep. Because he had been away from home for months, even a hopeful Frances knew what that meant. He had been unfaithful to her with many women. (Sting did not publicly comment on his fear of sexually transmitted diseases [STDs] from sleeping with so many women.)

Despite their troubles, the couple had another child together, Fuchsia Katherine, in April 1982. But by then Sting was already seriously involved with another woman, an actress named Trudie Styler. He and Frances were clearly headed for divorce.

Sting's Legal Troubles

In addition to the breakdown of his marriage and the inevitable divorce, Sting faced another legal battle in the summer of 1982 involving his old songwriting deal with Virgin Music. Miles Copeland had convinced Sting that the deal he had signed so many years ago was not only unfair but against the law.

His songs, which were earning Virgin millions, did not legally belong to him because of the contract he signed when he was struggling to make ends meet and could not afford a lawyer to review the contracts. Sting wanted his songs back and took the company to court. He was especially upset when the company sold the rights for "Don't Stand So Close to Me" for use in a deodorant commercial.

After two intense weeks, the case was eventually settled out of court, and both sides claimed victory. Sting got the rights to his songs back while Virgin had made plenty of money from them in the meantime. "My songs are like my children," Sting explained. "You want to protect them when they're being abused. I won the case because I will get my songs back."[23]

Frances had testified in court on behalf of her husband and his rights as a songwriter, but just weeks after the settlement, she and Sting separated. Not only had Sting had affairs for years, he now had a girlfriend he saw regularly.

And to make matters worse, Trudie, his girlfriend, had been Frances's friend. The two actresses had met and formed a friendship years earlier when Frances and Sting lived in their basement apartment. Trudie lived on one of the higher floors. Ironically, she had noticed Sting at the time too and thought he was handsome. Sting had been attracted to his neighbor as well, but they never struck up a relationship.

Trudie Styler

Few could have believed that Trudie would be Sting's mistress and, one day, his wife. She was not a classically beautiful woman as so many rock stars seemed to be drawn to. And like Sting, she started out as part of a very poor family.

Trudie was born on January 6, 1955, in Birmingham, England. Trudie's father was a farm laborer turned factory worker who had two other daughters and a wife to support in addition to Trudie. To make matters worse, when Trudie was just two years old, she was hit by a van and the exhaust pipe left scars all over her face.

Because her family could not afford to remove the scars with extra surgery, Trudie had to deal with the teasing of classmates on the playground when she was little. Still, she did not let the fact that she was disfigured stop her from wanting to become an actress.

When she was seventeen, Trudie ran away from home and headed for the famous acting town of Stratford-upon-Avon in England (a place made famous by playwright William Shakespeare). She found a job with a family who needed someone to care for their children. The family also happened to be theatrical and they helped Trudie lose her regional English accent and get started in show business. She knew what she wanted. She said: "I want to be a famous actress . . . and I will be. There is no failure in my terms."[24]

Eventually, Trudie saved up enough money to have her scars fixed (something she knew she would need to do if she was to succeed in the looks-oriented profession of acting). By the late 1970s, Trudie had had some success appearing on several television series. But she still had to take a job as a bunny girl (a cocktail waitress dressed up in a skimpy bunny outfit) at a London

Sting poses with his second wife, Trudie Styler, at the 2001 Golden Globe Awards. The two became lovers while Sting was still married to Frances.

nightclub to make ends meet. It was during this time that she befriended Frances and first noticed Sting who lived in the basement apartment of her building.

Two years later, Frances and Trudie even starred together in a stage version of *Macbeth*. The night that Sting came to see the show, Trudie bumped into him backstage and the two remembered one another. In fact, Sting could not get Trudie out of his thoughts. The two started a close friendship without Frances's knowledge and a short time later became lovers.

Just weeks after Sting announced his separation from Frances, Trudie went out on tour with him. Although she was in love with Sting, it was hard to be portrayed as a homewrecker by the media. She described the beginning of her relationship with Sting as "a very dark time [in which] we were put on trial."[25] It was hard on Sting too—suddenly the media had yet another reason to hound him.

"Stingola" and *Synchronicity*

Sting had not been out of the eye of the media since The Police had taken off. His band mates even had a name for the hype and hysteria he created wherever he went: "Stingola." Stewart Copeland said: "It works like this. A journalist comes on the road with the band to write a feature. I talk to him for hours. Andy talks to him for hours and Sting never says a word—except that just once, he walks through the room where I'm busy bending this guy's ear and he says, 'Where's the toilet?' And that's the headline!"[26]

Whereas all the Stingola had been focused only on Sting in the past, Trudie and Sting were suddenly at the center of a media whirlwind. They were constantly followed and photographed, which put a strain on their relationship from the start. Still, they stayed together. Sting seemed committed to the blonde actress and did not seek out attention from female fans as he had previously done. Trudie also seemed to have a positive effect on his drug use, which was becoming less frequent.

Meanwhile, the group was readying *Synchronicity*, their fifth album, for release. The breakup of Sting's marriage provided the fuel he needed to write so many songs based on pain, a feeling he says he needs to create his best work. Sting admits, "In the past, I've often suspected myself of manufacturing unhappiness. I didn't have that problem this time."[27]

The dark tone of the album did not dampen people's reaction to it. When it was released in the summer of 1983, it was an immediate hit. It topped the U.S. charts for an amazing seventeen weeks. "Every Breath You Take," the first single from *Synchronicity*, was equally successful. "I consider it a fairly nasty song," Sting explains. "It's about surveillance and ownership and jealousy."[28] Still, many saw it as a beautiful love song–maybe because they did not listen closely to the lyrics but thought the title and melody were sweet.

Other singles from the album included "King of Pain" and "Wrapped Around Your Finger." Stephen Holden of *Rolling Stone* called it "their finest album. . . . Even more than on the hauntingly ambient *Ghost in the Machine*, each cut on *Synchronicity* is not simply a song but a miniature, discreet soundtrack. *Synchronicity*'s biggest surprise, however, is the explosive and bitter passion of Sting's newest songs."[29]

Synchronicity was the group's most popular and acclaimed album to date–it would also be their last.

Quitting The Police

To promote the album, the group went back on the road again. This tour was considerably different from the ones in the band's early days. They now had an entourage and crew of nearly one hundred people, including publicists, security guards, makeup artists and hair stylists, costumers, and roadies to lug and set up all their equipment. Summers once admitted: "[We] had people working for us whose names we didn't even know."[30]

Luxury hotels awaited Sting, Copeland, and Summers, but the feel of touring had not changed for Sting. He said of touring in 1996:

> Sometimes I feel I could actually do without it, though it would be very difficult to find something else in my life that's like walking onto a stage in front of twenty thousand people who are all basically saying, "We're pleased to see you." That's a very powerful drug. Whether I could do without that, I'm not too sure. I get a different kind of at

The Price of Fame

During the Synchronicity tour, Sting realized that The Police had achieved the height of their popularity and could go no further.

tention from my family that's obviously more personal but just as intense. I'd say I enjoy playing live, but if there comes a time when it doesn't feel natural to be a performer, then I hope I have the courage and wisdom to stop."[31]

While Sting knew he would not quit performing, he was struggling with thoughts of whether or not he should quit The Police. He was tired of fighting and was even considering a career as an actor or solo musician instead. "The band is just one part of our lives," he said. "It's not the entire be-all and end-all of our lives. If it was that'd be awful. I couldn't stand it. I need a private life and I need private modes of expression."[32]

The answer to Sting's question as to whether he should leave came to him the night the group performed in front of the largest crowd it had ever commanded, at New York's Shea Stadium on August 18, 1983. Huge video monitors hung from the stadium walls so that even those in the back of the crowd could see the group's electrified performance. Everything was perfect that night. The group was performing perfectly and actually getting along. And, as if on cue, the moon rose above the stadium wall in the middle of the group's rendition of "Walking on the Moon."

The group was at the height of its popularity and had given an amazing performance. Sting decided right then and there that they should break up because, as he said, "[w]e were at the top. We could not get any higher."[33]

Miles Copeland disagreed with Sting and wanted them to stay together, even though he noticed that they had become more competitive. Summers was the only member of the group who thought that breaking up might have "been a little premature. We have continued to sell a lot of records and still do."[34]

Despite the feelings of Copeland and Summers, the group disbanded at the end of 1983. Publicly, the members claimed they were just taking a short break, and fans hoped they would be back in the recording studio soon. But each member knew what "the break" really meant. The Police was over.

Chapter 5

Musician Turned Actor

THE YEAR 1983 had been a difficult one for Sting. His separation from Frances turned into divorce and he was no longer part of a group, but Sting claimed he did not have regrets about the past. In 1985, he said:

> I'm grateful I went through the crisis. I worked hard to survive it. My best creative work so far [the *Synchronicity* album] is a result of trying to work out those problems. "Every Breath You Take" is a song about a man abandoned. I've never regretted either my success or my so-called falling apart. I'm also not one to make the same mistakes twice. I've learned what I've done wrong so far and at least I can make different mistakes next time.[35]

Although the members had disbanded, The Police made more money in 1983 than in any other year–thanks to the tremendous success of *Synchronicity*, which sold more than twelve million copies. In addition to the money the album brought in, critics considered it the band's best work and it won numerous awards, including four Grammy awards. The Police seemed to be at the top of their game, so there was amazement and confusion when the band broke up.

Sting, however, was relieved. He had laid the groundwork for a solo music career in 1982 when he had written and performed some solo tracks for films, and he had been acting since 1980. So he knew that he would be able to work despite no longer being part of The Police.

Sting's Kids

While Sting was worried that he was never a good husband to his first wife, he has always maintained that he was a great father. This is a good thing since between his two marriages Sting has six kids! His first child Joseph was born in 1976 and is now a musician himself.

Although Sting never helped his son break into the business, Joe did travel as a roadie with his dad and was introduced to some famous musicians. In 1993, he formed the Australian Nightmare, his first band, with some friends from school. Joe's career never took off as his father's did but he enjoys playing music today and is also a graphic artist.

Sting's other children are Fucshia Katherine (Kate) born in 1982, and four kids with wife Trudie: two girls (Mickey and Coco) and two boys (Jake and Giacomo Luke).

A friend of Sting's, who wished to remain anonymous, said in the biography *The Secret Life of Gordon Sumner* by Wensley Clarkson: "Sting is incredibly generous with his children but in a realistic way. He doesn't throw money at them but he tries to give each of them an equal amount of time so that none of them feel left out. I think he is one of the best fathers that I have ever met."

Trying Acting

Sting's first acting role had really been as part of The Police, when the band was cast in a Wrigley's chewing gum commercial. In 1978 he had also been cast in *The Great Rock 'n' Roll Swindle*, a film by the punk band The Sex Pistols, but his part had ended up on the cutting room floor. Sting's first taste at real acting was in 1979 in his film debut as a character in the movie *Quadrophenia*. The movie was the project of The Who's Pete Townshend and it developed a cult following as well as rave reviews at the Cannes Film Festival.

Sting suddenly had the attention of the acting world as well. But he was pretty modest about his acting abilities: "Looking good on screen is just a matter of intelligence. . . . I was lucky in [*Quadrophenia*] because I was in it just long enough to make an impression, but not long enough to blow it."[36]

Filmmakers agreed that he did not blow it and started offering Sting more parts. Sting was wisely selective about the ones he chose. He shied away from big-budget projects, turning down everything from films by famous director Francis Ford Coppola (of *The Godfather* fame) to a James Bond flick. He did have parts in the offbeat *Radio One*, *Artemis 81*, and *Brimstone and Treacle*. He also took a role as a villain in David Lynch's *Dune*. Sting traveled to Mexico for the film's five-month shoot in the spring of 1983. After he returned, Sting did not have much time to himself before he was off on the *Synchronicity* tour with The Police.

With all the touring and music making, he did not have much time to devote to his newfound interest in acting. But in 1984, the year that *Dune* was released, Sting suddenly had time on his hands. He had spent the past six years constantly working at music and had decided he wanted to reinvent himself. He wanted a change. He wanted to be an actor.

Luckily, Hollywood had not forgotten that Sting had great screen presence (both in films and in music videos), and Sting easily made the transition from music to movies. He said in September 1983: "They're [music and film] obviously related, and though music may have given me confidence that somewhat

Sting (right) is shown in a scene from Dune. *After leaving The Police, Sting decided to focus almost exclusively on his acting career.*

prepared me for being in front of the camera, making transitions is the hardest thing for a performer to do. And you know, you don't have to have the intelligence of a brain surgeon to play rock & roll. The opposite is the general rule, in fact."[37]

Leading Man

Sting had both the looks and the brains to be successful in the movies. Director Franc Roddam, who had first given Sting his small cameo role in *Quadrophenia*, approached him in 1984 about playing Dr. Frankenstein in his movie *The Bride*. "I didn't realize how good an actor he had become,"[38] Roddam said. He originally planned on offering Sting a small role rather than the lead, but changed his mind after he gave the thirty-three-year-old a screen test. "He can be a romantic lead and is able to play dark, dangerous evil parts. He's not afraid to die in a movie,"[39] Roddam raved.

Playing a lead in a major motion picture was hard work, but Sting managed it all and kept his ego in check for filming. Costar Jennifer Beals described him as "fun, sweet, supportive, and he doesn't isolate himself in any way."[40] There were rumors that Beals and Sting were having an offscreen love affair but both denied the rumors.

Instead of wooing his leading lady, Sting made it clear to the cast and crew that he was there to learn about the craft of acting. He showed up on time each day, knew his lines, and patiently waited on the set for his scenes. Sting also had some unique ideas about acting:

> At its worst in acting you are a coat hanger. At its best, though, there is an evocation of sympathy, a heightened glimpse of reality. Dr. Frankenstein makes the wrong decisions in the end, goes mad and is pure evil. He's like us all, a victim of circumstance, but the architect of his own doom. We're not here to be happy, we're here to learn. In acting you get to express all these pent-up emotions. You can kill, run over people, shoot, behave like a monster and work them out of your system.[41]

Musician Turned Actor 63

In his first leading role in The Bride, *Sting approached the part of Dr. Frankenstein with a great degree of professionalism.*

Unfortunately, reviews for *The Bride* were not glowing. An *Entertainment Weekly* video review said:

> *The Bride* . . . wallows in its pretensions, what with the fancy typestyle of the credits and the lush fruitiness of Maurice Jarre's score. Here, Frankenstein (Sting) concocts a mate for his creature (Clancy Brown, whose remarkable performance suggests a better movie), a "bride" seemingly assembled entirely from American corpses, without stitching–Jennifer Beals looks great and talks just like a Yale undergraduate. It's clear that Roddam was going for a gothic, Bronte-esque romance; what he got was a misshapen lump.[42]

Luckily, Sting had the opportunity to work with established actors on his next project *Plenty*, which he began filming just one day after finishing *The Bride*. Veteran actors Meryl Streep and Sir John Gielgud also starred in the film and Sting knew he would learn even more on this film. He was right. Reviews for the film were stellar and Sting was singled out for his performance as a man in love with Streep.

More screen roles followed, including *Julia and Julia* with Kathleen Turner and *The Grotesque* (also called *Gentlemen Don't*

Eat Poets and *Grave Indiscretion*), which also starred Trudie Styler. Sting proved he could really throw himself into a part when he was conducting research for his role in *The Grotesque*, in which he played a butler. Sting explained to a *People* magazine reporter:

> First I thought that I could just watch an Anthony Hopkins film because he makes such a good butler. Then I did one better, I hired the guy who taught Anthony how to buttle. . . . I answered the door. I checked on supper. This was all much to the delight of [Trudie]. Next thing you know, I'll be doing the cooking. . . . Now if music doesn't work out, I have a future. . . . I'd be expensive because I'd do a good job and I do have a certain lifestyle to maintain.[43]

Sting did take a cut in pay to act but he had made enough in music not to care about smaller checks. Plus, he was learning that there were other parts of filmmaking that intrigued him, including directing and screenwriting.

Screenwriting Radio Days

In addition to acting, Sting wanted to try his hand at writing for the screen. He had wanted to write a screenplay since his first days on tour with The Police. Sting purchased the rights to Melvyn Peaks's trilogy of gothic fantasy novels. He wrote *Gormenghast* as a vehicle for himself, and then set to work getting financing for it. He said:

> Knowing a lot of actors, I see that most of them sit by the phone waiting for jobs to come to them. Some of them get lucky, but most of them might as well wait for the lottery to come up. So I thought, "Okay, if I want to do a movie, I can afford to buy a property for me." So I bought the rights to these books. . . . When you're asking for $6 million or $7 million, people are frightened of giving it to you. Basically, you're dealing with people's personal anxieties when you try to get financing for a film. These people are sitting in their offices, smoking their cigars, and their jobs are very tentative. Still, that's no way to run an art form.[44]

Unsuccessful Reunions

Although The Police never formally announced their breakup until March 1985, the group's members knew it had been over for more than a year before that. The group played their last concert in January 1985 and then the members went their separate ways. But the guys were not done cashing in on their success together. Several greatest hits albums were released, as was a video (in addition to many illegal bootleg recordings from which the group did not profit).

The guys did reunite from time to time. They played together to benefit charity with Amnesty International in 1986. They also got together for a one-time performance in 1992 at Sting's wedding reception, but they had been drinking and did not really give a great performance. Sting recalled in the biography *Sting: Demolition Man*:

> We got up and we hadn't rehearsed or planned anything and we started with "Message in a Bottle" and Andy starts the riff, he can just about remember it; and Stewart immediately starts . . . speeding up, as usual . . . so I turn round and ten years just suddenly evaporate and there I am glowering at Stewart and he's glowering at me. Andy's fumbling with the chords and suddenly it's all come back and Stewart and I caught each other doing it and started to laugh. It was very funny. It was actually a very warm moment. The tension was back immediately. People said that the atmosphere was electric watching it.

Sting had trouble finding interest in his adaptation, so instead of producing *Gormenghast* for the screen he recorded it for the radio. He received great reviews for his dramatic reading and, buoyed by his success, decided that maybe he had a future as a stage actor.

Broadway Bound

Sting was not content just to act in films and write them, he also wanted to try his hand at Broadway, that famed and prestigious area of New York theaters. For years, Sting had been approached to do musicals but he had turned down the offers, claiming he did not want to be the next John Travolta (the actor who became known for his singing roles—as in *Grease*—in the 1970s and then had a career slump before a comeback in the 1990s).

Still, he had a hard time turning down an offer to appear in *The Threepenny Opera*. He liked the plot of the show because, he explained, "[i]t asks an important question: How can you get people to obey the rules of society when they don't have a stake in the society?"[45]

Unfortunately, the show opened in late 1989 to bad reviews and it closed just weeks into what was supposed to be a nineteen-week run. Sting's reviews as Machete, or Mack the Knife, were mixed, and Sting claimed he felt "like a giant moose on the first day of hunting season." Robert Bursting of the *New Republic* wrote:

Not satisfied with his work for the silver screen, Sting also wished to bring his dramatic talents to Broadway. Here, he appears as Mack the Knife in The Threepenny Opera.

> The celebrated rock singer Sting has shown acting talent in movies, and it's not his fault that he'd been so uncomfortably (and cynically) miscast. . . . Actually, he's rather sweet in the part, shy, retiring, even a little demure. Brecht wanted the character to be an aging predatory businessman with a paunch. Sting comes on like a modest English gentleman with a sword stick–Douglas Fairbanks, Jr. minus the swashbuckler.[46]

Still, Sting enjoyed the experience. A number of celebrities came to see Sting in his Broadway debut, including Jodie Foster and Glenn Close, and despite the reviews, he got standing ovations on several occasions. "He's having the time of his life," Sting's publicist said. "He didn't even go into this for reviews. He thought it would be a challenge."[47]

If there was anything Sting loved it was a challenge, and he was fast proving that he was up for anything interesting that came his way.

Chapter 6

Solo Pursuits

ACTING WAS SOMETHING Sting truly enjoyed and showed a talent for, but he could not deny his passion for music for very long. Less than a year after The Police broke up, Sting was readying himself for a solo musical career, which coincided with his acting career.

He had composed the soundtrack for his film *Brimstone and Treacle* and had previously recorded some songs alone. He finally felt it was time to be on his own and Sting knew just what type of music he wanted to pursue: his beloved jazz.

The Jazz Man

Jazz had been Sting's first love and he decided to return to it in January 1985, when he put out an open call for jazz musicians to back him up. Sting auditioned many musicians and chose four talented young African American men, including saxophonist Branford Marsalis, to accompany him on his first solo album, which he entitled *The Dream of the Blue Turtles*.

The title of the album was inspired by a dream Sting had in which blue turtles were climbing over the walls of his garden. The dream had also left him with the feeling that he should leave The Police, so the dream's theme became the title of his first solo album. He wrote many original and now well-known songs for the album, including "If You Love Somebody Set Them Free," "Shadows in the Rain," and "Fortress Around Your Heart," and changed his typical sound by adding riffs and extending chords.

Solo Pursuits

Sting performs with a jazz ensemble in the 1985 documentary Bring on the Night. *The film provides an intimate look at the making of* The Dream of the Blue Turtles *album.*

By September 1985, *The Dream of the Blue Turtles* was at the top of the charts and went platinum. The critics gave Sting their stamp of approval as well. "Sting can swing," wrote *Rolling Stone* critic Jon Pareles. "The new band is also punchier than the Police, because [Kenny] Kirkland's keyboards—especially the organ—reinforce the rhythm, and the [Omar] Hakim-[Darryl] Jones team packs a mighty wallop."[48] The album was even nominated for a Grammy Award in the jazz category.

Sting and the band also set off on a five-month tour. It felt good to Sting to be back on the road playing music. And he knew he wanted to continue.

Live Aid

It was a few more years before Sting had the time to work on another solo album. In the meantime, he donated his talents to a charity album called *Live Aid*. He joined many famous musicians in recording this album to benefit malnourished children in Africa.

In 1984, English documentary filmmaker Michael Burke made a striking film about the extreme hunger and starvation facing the people of Ethiopia. The people of England were shocked by the images of starving children and many wanted to help. Music maker

Bob Geldof organized a group of musicians to record a single called "Do They Know It's Christmas?/Feed the World." The group, which called themselves Band Aid, included more than forty English and Irish musicians. (U.S. musicians also had a single they produced the following year to help the starving in Ethiopia called "We Are the World.") "Do They Know It's Christmas?/Feed the World" went on to sell more than three million copies and became the best-selling record in the United Kingdom.

But members of Band Aid wanted to do more. They created *Live Aid*, a concert held on July 13, 1985, to benefit the famine victims. Some of the biggest names in music graced the stage at London's Wembley Stadium to raise more than $100 million. In the United States, musicians played at Philadelphia's JFK Stadium on the same day, and some performances were even shown in both countries via satellite.

In addition to Sting, the other world-famous performers included Adam Ant, INXS, Elvis Costello, The Hooters, Ozzy Osbourne and Black Sabbath, Phil Collins, Bryan Adams, Queen, The Pretenders, The Who, Elton John, and Paul McCartney.

Sting on His Life and Music

In May 1994, Sting donned a cap and gown again and received an honorary degree from the Berklee College of Music in Boston. Like Billy Joel and James Taylor before him, he was also the school's commencement speaker. As he addressed the crowd of graduates that day, he admitted to being nervous and gave those attending a rare glimpse into his life and songwriting. He showed that he had changed a lot since his music making days when he acted disdainfully to other musicians and had a large ego. In his speech that day, he said:

> There's been a lot written about my life. . . . I can't remember what's true and what isn't. I had no formal musical education. But I suppose I became successful by a combination of dumb luck, low cunning, and risk-taking born out of curiosity. I still operate in the same way. But your curiosity in music is never entirely satisfied. You could fill libraries with what I don't know about music. There's always something more to learn. . . . I can't even pretend to know. I've written hundreds of songs, had them published, had them in the charts. Grammys and enough written proof that I'm a bona fide, successful songwriter. Still, if somebody asks me how to write songs, I have to say, "I don't really know." I don't really know where they come from.

Going It Alone

In addition to donating his time to good causes, Sting was busy with acting, being a father, and assuring that his follow-up album was as successful and inspired as his first had been. During a particularly busy period for Sting in 1987, both of his parents (who had divorced years earlier) passed away from cancer. He was devastated, especially about the death of his mother with whom Sting was close and whom he credited for introducing him to music.

For the next three years, Sting suffered from writer's block and did not write any songs. In addition, he struggled with problems with his voice and throat that had plagued him since his early days with The Police, as well as difficulties with his hearing, which is gradually growing worse each year. (Sting has tinnitus, which is a ringing in the ears caused by damage from several things, including loud music, to the delicate parts of the ear.)

When Sting finally wrote and completed his new album *Soul Cages* in 1991, his musical style had changed and matured due to his losses. This album is about death. He wrote the songs on the album in just three weeks and dedicated it to his father–even though they had never been close, they reconciled before Ernie's death.

Sting's friends and fans alike noticed the change in mood and tone of *Soul Cages* and with his following albums *Ten Summoner's Tales* (1993) and *Mercury Falling* (1996), as well as a change in Sting himself. Friend and musician Branford Marsalis said:

> Sting was one of those road guys. We'd be on the road for a year and a half straight, and it was easier to do that than confront the demons. But I think the deaths of his parents really put him in a place where he had to confront some [stuff] about himself. . . . When I went to record with him, he was so peaceful . . . that it really touched me. Now, even his songs that are light still deal with a certain amount of depth and a certain level of mortality.[49]

Jazz saxophonist Branford Marsalis poses with his instrument. Marsalis lent Sting's early solo projects a distinctly jazzy tone.

Critics also noticed the change in Sting and generally rewarded him for it with rave reviews. Critic Jon Pareles in a review appearing in *Rolling Stone* called *Soul Cages* "searing," and for *Ten Summoner's Tales* he said Sting was "a riveting singer, easily one of the best on the contemporary scene–and sending his mind and heart few places stars risk, Sting proves with 'Ten Summoner's Tales,' that even when he's not going for credos, his abiding concerns are significant and moving."[50] Pareles saw Sting perform songs from *Mercury Falling* at a club in Manhattan before the album's release and tour. Sting told the crowd that there might be mistakes in the set, but Pareles claims that "[d]espite Sting's warnings, the music was in fine shape."[51]

Many critics had doubted whether Sting would have solo success comparable to what he had had with The Police. But he proved that he was an even more formidable force as a solo musician.

Solo Pursuits 73

Sting had always been a perfectionist and he seemed to be even more selective about his work as he grew older. One example was with his 1999 album *Brand New Day*, the most celebrated and biggest-selling album (it sold more than seven million copies) of his solo career. Sting states: "I composed, finessed, and even sequenced [decided the order of the songs on

Q & A With Sting

Despite the fact that he has been in the media spotlight for more than two decades, Sting has remained a mystery to many. In July 2000, Sting sat down with a *Vanity Fair* reporter and answered some unusual questions:

Q: (*Vanity Fair*): What is your greatest fear?

A: (Sting): Fear itself.

Q: Which living person do you most admire?

A: Nelson Mandela.

Q: What is your greatest extravagance?

A: My home.

Q: What is your favorite journey?

A: Home.

Q: On what occasion do you lie?

A: Only when absolutely necessary.

Q: What or who is the greatest love of your life?

A: My wife.

Q: What do you consider your greatest achievement?

A: My family.

Q: What is your most treasured possession?

A: My mental and physical health.

Q: What do you value most in your friends?

A: Honesty, intelligence, and humor.

Q: Who is your favorite hero of fiction?

A: Huckleberry Finn. [The main character in Mark Twain's *The Adventures of Huckleberry Finn*.]

Q: What is your motto?

A: "Die without fear."

Q: When and where were you happiest?

A: Right here, right now.

the album] the music before I'd ever written a word. I had to trust that the music would tell me stories, begin to create characters. It's almost a mysterious process. You have to be patient. It's a little like sculpting wood–you begin to see them in the wood."[52]

Sting's new approach to songwriting came with a newfound feeling toward life: happiness. Sting had a solid relationship with Trudie, healthy children, an amazing career, and more money than he could ever spend. He said in 1996:

> I used to believe very strongly that in order to write anything worthwhile, you needed to be in some sort of crisis. And I would manufacture crises in order to be able to write. I was that sick, and I wasn't alone; a lot of people still believe that. So I made a conscious decision in my life to say, "Well, I've worked hard enough to deserve to be happy and still be creative and not in some kind of emotional turmoil." And I think I've proved that that can be done.[53]

Part of Sting's happiness was due to the healthy lifestyle to which he had adapted. No longer a young and reckless rock star, Sting gave up drugs, drank minimally, meditated and exercised daily, and ate well. Despite the fact that he was getting older, Sting looked and felt better than he had in years.

Sting Gets Married

On August 20, 1992, nearly a decade to the day after they started dating, Sting and Trudie made their relationship official by getting married near their north London home. They already had three children together and were seen as a married couple. Still, prior to that day they were not legally married. The marriage ceremony itself was brief, low-key, and laid-back.

But on August 22, the newly married couple had a more formal church service for 250 guests at St. Andrew's Church in England. Trudie wore an expensive ivory wedding gown by designer Gianni Versace, while Sting wore tails and a black-and-white striped vest. The couple's children, as well as the two from Sting's previous marriage, acted as attendants.

Solo Pursuits

Sting married Trudie Styler nearly ten years after they started dating. Here, the couple attends a memorial Mass for Gianni Versace with Princess Diana and Elton John.

Guests were treated to an elaborate reception that included a Police reunion. They were generous in return: Keith Moore, Sting's accountant and manager, gave them a Jaguar while Miles Copeland gave them a beautiful four-poster bed. Guests partied until the early hours of the morning and were treated to a barbecue the following day.

Accountant Stings Sting

But it was not all happiness for Sting. In the 1980s, Sting had claimed he did not have a head for business. But with all the millions coming his way as his career progressed, Sting made it a point to learn about managing his money. Unfortunately, Keith Moore, the person Sting entrusted to manage his money full time, did not deserve his trust, as he had embezzled more than $9 million from Sting over the fifteen years that he worked for the musician.

According to *Billboard* magazine, Moore began transferring money from a bank account held by Sting's company Steerpike Overseas, Ltd. (which Sting had formed with Frances, his first wife, and now partnered with Trudie). This money was moved into two accounts in Moore's name, and he used it to fund a number of personal endeavors (including converting Russian military aircraft for civilian use and setting up some restaurants), as well as to help himself avoid bankruptcy.

Moore's actions were revealed in an anonymous letter sent by someone in his office. Sting was outraged and believed that he now had no money. But of course, the reason the missing $9 million had not been noticed was because it was only a small dent in Sting's fortune.

Moore insisted that he had Sting's permission for taking some of the money. Sting claimed that he was not that generous an employer. The court believed Sting, and Moore was found guilty. He was sentenced to six years in prison.

Solo Awards

In addition to all the number-one hits he has had over the years, Sting has received numerous honors for his musical endeavors. He won many Grammy awards with The Police and even more as a solo artist. He was inducted into the National Academy of Popular Music's Songwriters Hall of Fame.

Sting and Trudie are also regular fixtures at the Academy Awards. This could be because Sting's original songs that are used

Sting poses proudly with a pair of Grammys at the 2000 awards show. The performer has won a number of distinctions throughout his career for his unique brand of music.

in films, like *The Emperor's New Groove* and *Kate & Leopold*, are often nominated for awards. Despite performing at the ceremonies, Sting has yet to walk away with an Academy Award for himself.

But unlike many musicians, Sting's awards extend beyond those dedicated solely to music. He was awarded a star on Hollywood's Walk of Fame and his humanitarian work has earned him even more recognition and awards.

Sting, the Activist and Humanitarian

Sting had always been interested in politics and human rights. He had no problem donating his time and money to *Live Aid* and considered it an honor to play for such a good cause. But it was not until he learned about the gradual deforestation of the Brazilian rain forests that Sting really threw himself into supporting something about which he cared so passionately. Sting has been committed to helping save and protect this precious area of jungle since December 1987. He was in Rio de Janeiro, Brazil, when he agreed to take a tour of the jungle with Belgian photographer Jean-Pierre Dutilleux who had made an Academy Award–nominated documentary about the plight of the rain forests, which are facing deforestation.

Sting was feeling especially vulnerable during his first trip to meet the Indian tribe that lived in the rain forests. His father had just passed away and he spent much of the visit wearing dark glasses to hide his red, teary eyes. But the trip was incredibly worthwhile and Sting realized that he wanted to do everything he could to preserve the natural beauty of the rain forests and the way of life of the people there. This trip changed his life and has remained close to his heart for years. Over the past decade, Sting has returned to the Brazilian rain forests several times.

In addition to his visits, Sting has done work to benefit the rain forests through Amnesty International. He also took friend Chief Raoni on a world tour with him to spread awareness of the destruction of the rain forests. Sting's Rainforest Foundation has raised over $1 million to preserve 150,000 square miles of the forest.

Although Sting's efforts have been rewarded with saving land and winning awards for his tireless efforts, he has also been criticized for his work. In 1990, Sting's efforts came under fire

Sting talks with Chief Raoni (far left) and other members of the Menkragnoti Kayapo tribe of the Amazon. Sting has long used his celebrity status to draw attention to political and environmental issues.

when a British television program said that most of the money raised by Sting had gone toward the foundation's administrative costs while precious little of the money was going to the Indians or the rain forests. Sting was upset by the accusations and hired legal counsel to clear up the confusion. He eventually got the matter settled and his name was cleared.

Today, most people are aware of Sting's efforts on behalf of and love for the rain forest.

Sting's "Desert Rose"

Brand New Day, released in 1999, is undoubtedly Sting's most popular solo album to date and its single "Desert Rose" became an enormous hit.

He said in an article on his official website on the eve of his U.S. tour:

> It's an unusual song. . . . It begins with Cheb Mami singing in Arabic, which people were very afraid of at first; they thought it would be an impossible task getting that on the radio. (The ads) opened the floodgates really;

Solo Pursuits

once people recognized the song, radio was much more amenable, and we ended up playing the Super Bowl! I know people may feel that you're cashing in, or you're playing the game too . . . earnestly. But it just seemed an opportunity I was willing to take, and I'm glad we did it. But I don't think you'd find my songs selling hard liquor or cigarettes or anything like that.[54]

Sting's Style

Musically, Sting is constantly reinventing himself, and while many people love that about him, some have had their criticisms. Sting told reporter David Furnish of *Interview* magazine in 1996:

> I've been criticized for being too stylistically diverse since going solo, but it has become my thing. I've become my own category, which maybe I should escape from. Having succeeded at one thing, I feel the need to move on to the next stage, even if I'm not sure what that is. The more I learn about music composition, for instance, the

Sting performs his hit "Desert Rose" with Algerian star Cheb Mami at the 2000 Grammy Awards. The song represents the first mainstream duet between European and Arabic performers.

more I realize I don't know. It's an onion, and you keep on peeling it. I think rock 'n' roll is very reactionary and conservative in a way. It decides that there's these three or four chords and that's it, it doesn't grow. I mean, I like rock 'n' roll, but it's a closed system. . . . I want an open-ended system, which I think is more modern. Serious modern music is about having no limitations. No one knows where it's going but it's going somewhere. Popular music can have a feeling, too, or at least it should have.[55]

The Future

Sting had once claimed that he would not be a rock star after the age of thirty-five, but he has clearly changed his mind about that and shows no sign of slowing down. He is usually the first musician to donate his time to a good cause, including singing a version of his single "Fragile" at a telethon to benefit families whose loved ones died in the terrorist tragedies of September 11, 2001, in New York City, Washington, D.C., and Pennsylvania.

As musician, actor, and humanitarian, Sting has touched the lives of many all over the world.

He is also working on his memoirs. The autobiography is set to be released in the fall of 2004. Fans are anxious to get a better look into the life of this complicated, mysterious, and even contradictory artist.

Sting realizes how lucky he has been to have such a long and successful career, and to be his own person, making his own choices along the way. "I've always managed to do exactly what I wanted," he says, "and largely it's collided with popular tastes."[56] Maybe that is because, with his unique style and innovative musical offerings, Sting has largely created popular taste through the years. His millions of fans would certainly say this is so, and they cannot wait to hear what comes next.

Notes

Introduction: An Englishman on the Charts
1. Quoted in Jeff Clark-Meads, "Sting," *Vanity Fair*, July 2000, p. 200.
2. Quoted in Kristine McKenna, "A Monster Called Sting," *Rolling Stone*, September 1, 1983, p. 13.
3. Quoted in Sting biography, Steerpike Overseas Ltd. 2001. www.sting.com.

Chapter 1: Humble Beginnings
4. Quoted in McKenna, "A Monster Called Sting," p. 14.
5. Quoted in Christopher Sandford, *Sting: Demolition Man*. New York: Carroll and Graf Publishers, 1998, p. 18.
6. Quoted in McKenna, "Monster Called Sting," p. 14.
7. Quoted in *MacLean's*, "An Englishman on Tour," August 26, 1996, p. 38.
8. Quoted in McKenna, "A Monster Called Sting," p. 15.
9. Sting's Commencement Address at Berklee College of Music, May 15, 1994. www.berklee.edu.
10. Quoted in Wensley Clarkson, *The Secret Life of Gordon Sumner*. New York: Thunder's Mouth Press, 1995, p. 6.
11. Quoted in David Furnish, "Rock's Bach," *Interview*, July 1996, p. 92.
12. Quoted in Furnish, "Rock's Bach," p. 92.
13. Clarkson, *Secret Life of Gordon Sumner*, p. 21.

Chapter 2: Finding His Way
14. Quoted in Clarkson, *Secret Life of Gordon Sumner*, pp. 29–30.
15. Quoted in Clarkson, *Secret Life of Gordon Sumner*, p. 38.
16. Quoted in Clarkson, *Secret Life of Gordon Sumner*, pp. 44–45.

Chapter 3: Sting and The Police

17. Quoted in Sandford, *Sting*, p. 43.
18. Quoted in McKenna, "A Monster Called Sting," p. 12.
19. Quoted in Clarkson, *Secret Life of Gordon Sumner*, p. 70.
20. Quoted in McKenna, "A Monster Called Sting," p. 13.

Chapter 4: The Price of Fame

21. Quoted in McKenna, "A Monster Called Sting," p. 16.
22. www.rollingstone.com.
23. Quoted in Clarkson, *Secret Life of Gordon Sumner*, p. 144.
24. Quoted in Clarkson, *Secret Life of Gordon Sumner*, p. 147.
25. Quoted in Sandford, *Sting*, p. 116.
26. Quoted in Clarkson, *Secret Life of Gordon Sumner*, p. 118.
27. Quoted in Sandford, *Sting*, p. 139.
28. Stephen Holder. www.rollingstone.com.
29. Quoted in Sandford, *Sting*, p. 141.
30. Quoted in Sandford, *Sting*, p. 140.
31. Quoted in Furnish, "Rock's Bach," p. 93.
32. Quoted in Clarkson, *Secret Life of Gordon Sumner*, p. 144.
33. Quoted in Clarkson, *Secret Life of Gordon Sumner*, p. 156.
34. Quoted in Clarkson, *Secret Life of Gordon Sumner*, p. 161.

Chapter 5: Musician Turned Actor

35. Quoted in Jim Jerome, "Sting's the Thing!" *People Weekly*, January 14, 1985, p. 94.
36. Quoted in Sandford, *Sting*, p. 80.
37. Quoted in McKenna, "A Monster Called Sting," p. 17.
38. Quoted in Jerome, "Sting's the Thing!" p. 92.
39. Quoted in Jerome, "Sting's the Thing!" p. 92.
40. Quoted in Jerome, "Sting's the Thing!" p. 93.
41. *Entertainment Weekly*, "The Bride: Mary Shelley's Frankenstein; Bram Stoker's Dracula; The Bride; The Doctor and the Devils; The Company of Wolves," April 28, 1995. www.ew.com.
42. Quoted in Jerome, "Sting's the Thing!" p. 94.
43. Quoted in Chuck Arnold, "How to Hustle Your Buttle," *People Weekly*, March 17, 1997, p. 120.
44. Quoted in McKenna, "A Monster Called Sting," p. 16.

45. Quoted in Jeff Clark-Meads, "Threepenny Opera, Critics Claim Ain't Got a Thing If It's Still Got That Sting," *People Weekly*, November 20, 1989, p. 77.
46. Quoted in Robert Bursting, "The Threepenny Opera," *The New Republic*, December 11, 1989, p. 29.
47. Quoted in Clark-Meads, "Threepenny Opera," p. 77.

Chapter 6: Solo Pursuits

48. Jon Pareles. www.rollingstone.com.
49. Quoted in Chris Willman, "King of Painlessness," *Entertainment Weekly*, August 9, 1996, p. 34.
50. Jon Pareles, "Pop Review: Understated Showcase for Sting's New Songs," *New York Times*, March 4, 1996. query.nytimes.com.
51. Pareles, "Pop Review."
52. www.sting.com.
53. Quoted in Willman, "King of Painlessness," p. 30.
54. www.sting.com.
55. Quoted in Furnish, "Rock's Bach," p. 93.
56. www.sting.com.

Important Dates in the Life of Sting

1951
Gordon Matthew Sumner is born to Ernest and Audrey Sumner in Wallsend, Newcastle upon Tyne, England.

1959–1960
Discovers the guitar his uncle has left behind at his house and becomes obsessed with learning to play it.

1970
Graduates from St. Cuthbert's Grammar School and takes a series of odd jobs before going to a teachers college the following year.

1971
Starts playing in local musical groups.

1976
Marries Frances Tomelty and has a baby son named Joseph; gets songwriting deal with Virgin Music.

1977
Moves to London and joins The Police.

1978
The Police record their first album, *Outlandos d'Amour* and tour the United States; first hit single, "Roxanne," is released.

1979
The group tours the United States again and releases its second album, *Reggatta de Blanc*; The Police sell five million singles and two million albums.

1980
The Police begin a whirlwind tour and releases their third album, *Zenyatta Mondatta*; Sting films his first television movie, *Artemis 81*.

1981
Fourth album, *Ghost in the Machine,* is released; The Police earn a Grammy.

1982
Sting sues Virgin Music and wins back rights to the songs he has written; daughter Fuchsia Katherine (Kate) is born; separates from Frances; starts dating Trudie Styler; has first solo musical hit.

1983
Stars in *Dune*; The Police's fifth and last album, *Synchronicity*, is released; The Police break up.

1984
Daughter Brigitte Michael (Mickey) is born to Trudie and Sting; Sting makes back-to-back films.

1985
Records first solo album, *The Dream of the Blue Turtles*.

1986
Son Jake is born.

1987
Records second solo album, *Nothing Like the Sun*; both his parents pass away; first visits to the Brazilian rain forests.

1989
Coauthors book entitled *Jungle Stories*; stars in *The Threepenny Opera*.

1990
Daughter Eliot Paulina (Coco) is born.

1991
Third solo album, *Soul Cages,* is released.

1992
Trudie and Sting marry after a decade of being together.

1993
Fourth solo album, *Ten Summoner's Tales,* is released.

1995
Son Giacomo Luke is born.

1996
Fifth solo album, *Mercury Falling,* is released.

1999
Sixth solo album, *Brand New Day,* is released; Sting wins two Grammy awards.

2001
Sting performs his single "Fragile" at a benefit for families who lost loved ones in the September 11 tragedies.

For Further Reading

Books

Susan Maloney Clinton, *Live Aid (Cornerstones of Freedom)*. New York: Childrens Press, 1993. A book about the cultural phenomenon of *Live Aid*.

Stuart A. Kallen, ed., *The 1980s (Cultural History of the United States through the Decades)*. San Diego: Lucent Books, 1999. A look at what happened in the 1980s in politics, entertainment, cultural events, and so on.

Tom McGrath, *MTV: The Making of a Revolution*. Philadephia: Running Press, 1996. This book describes the rise of music television, how it became a big business, and how it changed pop culture.

Chris Salewicz and Adrian Boot, *Reggae Explosion: The Story of Jamaican Music*. New York: Harry N. Abrams, 2001. Provides an in-depth look at the history of reggae music.

Nicholas Schaffner, *The British Invasion: From the First Wave to the New Wave*. New York: McGraw-Hill, 1982. This book describes the musicians who came out of England between 1962 and 1982.

Timothy Whitmore, *An Introduction to Tropical Rain Forests*. New York: Oxford University Press, 1998. Describes rain forest biology and the importance of rain forests, including a geologic and ecologic overview.

Periodicals

David Furnish, "Rock's Bach," *Interview*, July 1996.

Jim Jerome, "Sting's the Thing!" *People Weekly*, January 14, 1985.

Kristine McKenna, "A Monster Called Sting," *Rolling Stone*, September 1, 1983.

Websites

Sting Official Website: www.sting.com.

Melanie Gold's Sting Site: www.suite101.com.

Sting etc.: www.stingetc.com.

Sting Us: www.stingus.net.

Works Consulted

Books

Wensley Clarkson, *The Secret Life of Gordon Sumner*. New York: Thunder's Mouth Press, 1995. An in-depth look at the life of Sting.

Christopher Sandford, *Sting: Demolition Man*. New York: Carroll and Graf Publishers, 1998. A biography covering the many different aspects of Sting's life.

Periodicals

Chuck Arnold, "How to Hustle Your Buttle," *People Weekly*, March 17, 1997.

Robert Bursting, "The Threepenny Opera," *The New Republic*, December 11, 1989.

Jeff Clark-Meads, "Sting Is Stung by Accountant for $9 Million," *Billboard*, October 28, 1995.

___, "Threepenny Opera, Critics Claim, Ain't Got a Thing If It's Still Got That Sting," *People Weekly*, November 20, 1989.

___, "Sting," *Vanity Fair*, July 2000.

Entertainment Weekly, "The Bride: Mary Shelley's Frankenstein; Bram Stoker's Dracula; The Bride; The Doctor and the Devils; The Company of Wolves," April 28, 1995.

MacLean's, "An Englishman on Tour," August 26, 1996.

Chris Willman, "King of Painlessness," *Entertainment Weekly*, August 9, 1996.

Internet Sources

Dave DiMartino, Sting Biography. launch.yahoo.com.

Jon Pareles, "Pop Review: Understated Showcase for Sting's New Songs," *New York Times*, March 4, 1996. query.nytimes.com.

——"Sting: The Dream of the Blue Turtles," *Rolling Stone*. www.rollingstone.com.

Sting's Commencement Address at Berklee College of Music, May 15, 1994. www.berklee.edu.

Index

A&M Records, 42
Academy Awards, 76–77
Adam Ant, 70
Adams, Bryan, 70
Addams Family, The (television show), 13
Amnesty International, 65, 77
Animals the, 18, 38
Artemis 81 (film), 61
Australian Nightmare, 60

Band Aid, 70
BBC, 17
Beals, Jennifer, 62-63
Beatles, 10, 17, 19, 25
"Bed's Too Big Without You, The," 47
Beethoven, 71
Berklee College of Music, 16–17, 70
Billboard (magazine), 75
Black Sabbath, 70
Bond, James, 61
Brand New Day (album), 73–74, 78–79
Bride, The (film), 62–63
Brimstone and Treacle (film), 61
Broadway, 65–67
Brown, Clancy, 63
Buggles, The, 44
Burdon, Eric, 38
Burke, Michael, 79
Bursting, Robert, 66

Cannes Film Festival, 60
"Can't Stand Losing You," 45
Cherry Vanilla, 37
Clapton, Eric, 38

Clarkson, Wensley, 60
Clash, The, 34
Close, Glenn, 67
Club a Go Go, 18
Collins, Phil, 70
Copeland, Miles
    advises Sting on Virgin contract, 52
    becomes manager of The Police, 41–42
    disapproves of drugs, 48
    gift given to Sting by, 75
    as mediator between Stewart and Sting, 51
Copeland, Stewart
    asks Sting to join Police, 35
    goes blond, 40
    musical style of, 47
    plays at Sting's wedding reception, 65
    problems between Sting and, 51
    reaction to media's attention of Sting, 44
Coppola, Francis Ford, 60
Costello, Elvis, 70
Cowell, Audrey. *See* Sumner, Audrey
Cream, 19
Curved Air, 35

Damned, 34
"De Do Do Do, De Da Da Da," 47
"Desert Rose," 78–79
"Don't Stand So Close to Me," 47, 53
"Do They Know It's Christmas?/Feed the World," 70
Dream of the Blue Turtles, The (album), 68–69
Dune (film), 61
Dutilleux, Jean-Pierre, 77

Index

Earthrise, 23
Emperor's New Groove, The (animated film), 77
"Every Breath You Take," 59
"Every Little Thing She Does is Magic," 51

Finn, Huckleberry, 73
"Fortress Around Your Heart," 68
Foster, Jodie, 67
"Fragile," 80
Frankenstein, Dr., 62–63
Furnish, David, 14, 79

Geldof, Bob, 70
Gentlemen Don't Eat Poets. See Grotesque, The
Ghost in the Machine (album), 50, 56
Gielgud, John, 63
Godfather, The (film), 61
Gong, 37
Gormenghast (radio broadcast), 64–65
Graham Bond Organization, 19
Grammy Awards, 59, 76
Grave Indiscretion. See Grotesque, The
Grease (play and film), 65
Great Rock 'n' Roll Swindle, The (film), 60
Grotesque, The (film), 63-64

Hakim, Omar, 69
Hedley, John, 26
Hendrix, Jimi, 19
Hooters, The, 70

"(If You Love Somebody) Set Them Free," 68
Interview (magazine), 14, 79
INXS, 70
IRA. *See* Irish Republican Army
Irish Republican Army (IRA), 29
Ivanhoe (Scott), 12

Jarre, Maurice, 63
jazz, 68–69
JFK Stadium, 70
Joel, Billy, 70
John, Elton, 70
Jones, Darryl, 69
Joseph and the Amazing Technicolor Dreamcoat (play), 26

Julia and Julia (film), 63

Kate & Leopold (film), 77
Kirkland, Kenny, 69
Koestler, Arthur, 50

Last Exit, 26-27, 30-31, 33, 35
Lerner and Lowe, 17
Lewis, Jerry Lee, 17
Little Richard, 17
Live Aid (album), 69–70, 77
London, 33-35
Lynch, David, 61

Machete, 66
Mack the Knife, 66
Mami, Cheb, 78
Manfred Mann, 19
Marley, Bob, 38
Marsalis, Branford, 68, 71
McCartney, Paul, 70
McKenna, Kristine, 30
Mercury Falling (album), 71–72
"Message in a Bottle," 44, 65
Miller, Agnes, 27
Miller, Glenn, 17, 37
Mingus, Charles, 19
Monk, Thelonious, 19
Moore, Keith, 75–76
Mozart, 17
MTV. *See* Music Television
Music Television (MTV), 44–45

National Academy of Popular Music's Songwriters Hall of Fame, 76
New Republic (magazine), 66
Newcastle Big Band, 24–26
Northern Counties Teacher Training College, 22

"One World," 51
Osbourne, Ozzy, 70
Outlandos d'Amour (album), 41

Padovani, Henri, 37–38
Pareles, Joe, 69, 72
Peak, Melvyn, 64
Pearson, Ronnie, 26, 30–31

People (magazine), 64
Phoenix, 23–24
Pink Floyd, 19
Plenty (film), 63
Police Around the World (documentary), 49
Police, The
   albums, numbers sold, 17, 45
     see also names of specific albums
   appears in Wrigley's chewing gum commercial, 39–40, 60
   awards won by, 59, 76
   birth of, 37–39
   breaks up, 56–58, 65
   first trip to United States by, 42–43
   growth of success of, 43–45
   Miles Copeland becomes manager of, 41-42
   popularity of, in punk clubs, 34
   problems among members of, 46–47, 49
   reunions of, 65, 73
Presley, Elvis, 17
Pretenders, 70
punk music, 34

Quadrophenia (film), 60, 62
Queen, 70

Radio On (film), 61
Rainforest Foundation, 77-78
Raoni, Chief, 77
reggae, 34, 38
Reggatta de Blanc (album), 44, 47
Richardson, Gerry, 23, 26–27, 30, 37
Rock Nativity (Christmas play), 27
Roddam, Franc, 62–63
Rodgers and Hammerstein, 17
Rolling Stone (magazine), 30, 47, 69, 72
Rolling Stones, 17
"Roxanne," 40–42, 45

San Sebastian Music Festival, 26
Saturday Night Live (television show), 40
Scott, Sir Walter, 12
Secret Life of Gordon Sumner, The (Clarkson), 60
Sedaka, Neil, 38
Selassie, Haile, 38

Sex Pistols, The, 34, 60
"Shadows in the Rain," 68
Shakespeare, William, 54
Shea Stadium, 57-58
Sid Vicious, 34
Simon, Paul, 38
Soul Cages (album), 71–72
"Spirits in the Material World," 51
St. Andrew's Church, 74
St. Cuthbert's Grammar School, 14
Steerpike Overseas Ltd., 75
Stevenson, Robert Louis, 12
Sting
   as activist and humanitarian, 77–78
   Beatles' influence on, 17
   birth of, 10
   career of
     as actor, 59–67
     awards won by, 76–77
     coping with fame, 47–50
     with Earthrise, 23
     enrolls in teacher's college, 22
     with Last Exit, 26–27, 30–31, 33, 35
     as model, 36
     Moore embezzles money from, 75–76
     musical style of, 79–0
     with Newcastle Big Band, 24–26
     odd jobs held after high school by, 21–22
     with Phoenix, 23–24
     receives honorary degree, 70
     as solo artist, 68–74, 78–79
     sues Virgin, 52-53
     as teacher, 27
   childhood of, 10–12
     as athlete, 15
     becomes interested in music, 16–19
     education of, 12–15
     experiments with drugs and sex, 15–16
     problems between parents and, 19–20, 22
   considers becoming a priest, 14
   drug and alcohol problems of, 48, 50
   as father, 60
   fitness obsession of, 49
   health problems of, 71
   marriages of, 27–30, 51–52, 74

Index

origin of nickname of, 23-24
parents of, die, 70
views of
  on politics, 30
  on touring, 56-57
  on United States, 43
Sting: Demolition Man (biography), 65
Stingola, 55-56
St. Paul's First School, 27
Streep, Merryl, 63
Styler, Trudie (wife), 53-55, 64, 74-75
Summers, Andy
  goes blond, 40
  joins Police, 38
  musical style of, 47
  plays at Sting's wedding reception, 65
  on Police's band crew, 56
  reaction to media's attention of Sting, 44
Sumner, Angela (sister), 12
Sumner, Anita (sister), 12
Sumner, Audrey (mother), 10-12, 16-18, 20
Sumner, Coco (daughter), 60
Sumner, Ernie (father), 10-12, 18-20, 22, 71
Sumner, Frances (wife)
  befriends Trudie, 55
  marital problems of, 51-53, 69
  marries Sting, 27-30
  moves to London, 32-33, 35-36
Sumner, Fuchsia Katherine (daughter), 52, 60
Sumner, Giacomo Luke (son), 60
Sumner, Gordon Matthew. *See* Sting
Sumner, Jake (son), 60
Sumner, Joseph "Joe" (son), 29, 51, 60
Sumner, Mickey (daughter), 60
Sumner, Philip (brother), 12, 15

Synchronicity (album), 55-56, 59, 61
Tafari, Ras, 38
Taylor, James, 19, 23, 70
Ten Summoner's Tales (album), 71-72
Threepenny Opera, The (play), 66-67
tinnitus, 71
Tomelty, Frances. *See* Sumner, Frances
Townshend, Pete, 60
Travolta, John, 65
Treasure Island (Stevenson), 12
Turner, Kathleen, 63

UB40, 38

Vanity Fair (magazine), 73
Versace, Gianni, 74
"Video Killed the Radio Star," 44
Virgin, 33, 35-36, 52-53

Wailers, 38
Walk of Fame, 77
"Walking on the Moon," 47, 50
Wallsend, 9-12
Warwick University, 21
"We Are the World," 70
Webber, Andrew Lloyd, 26
Wembley Stadium, 70
"When the World Is Running Down, You Make the Best of What's Still Around," 47
"Whispering Voices," 26
Who, The, 60, 70
Wilson, Carol, 33
Wrigley's chewing gum, 39-40, 60

yoga, 49

Zenyatta Mondatta (album), 47

Picture Credits

Cover Photo: Reuters Newmedia Inc./CORBIS
© Associated Press, AP, 32, 54, 75, 78, 79
© Associated Press, Fashion Wire Daily, 76
© Associated Press, Pool, 8
© Bettmann/CORBIS, 13
© CORBIS, 24, 36, 39
© Rufus F. Folkks/CORBIS, 80
© Lynn Goldsmith/CORBIS, 41
© Hulton/Archive by Getty Images, 22, 28, 48, 52
© London Aerial Photo Library/CORBIS, 9
Photofest, 6, 18, 25, 43, 57, 61, 63, 66, 69, 72
© Neal Preston/CORBIS, 34
© Denis O'Reagan/CORBIS, 46

About the Author

Award-winning author Anne E. Hill has written a dozen biographies and fiction novels for middle and teen readers, including two others for Lucent's People in the News series: *Sandra Bullock* and *Drew Barrymore*. Some of her other nonfiction titles include *Gwyneth Paltrow*, *Cameron Diaz*, and *Denzel Washington*.

A freelance writer for over five years, Hill graduated magna cum laude with a B.A. in English from Franklin and Marshall College in 1996, where she was a member of the Phi Beta Kappa honors society and wrote for the *Franklin and Marshall Magazine*. She lives outside Philadelphia, with her husband George and son Caleb. Her favorite Sting songs are "Fragile" and "Desert Rose."